Blog INC.

BLOGGING FOR PASSION, PROFIT, AND TO CREATE COMMUNITY

Joy Deangdeelert Cho

Edited by Meg Mateo Ilasco
Foreword by Grace Bonney

CHRONICLE BOOKS
SAN FRANCISCO

Library of Congress Cataloging-in-Publication Data:

Cho, Joy Deangdeelert.

  Blog, Inc. : blogging for passion, profit, and to create community / Joy Deangdeelert Cho ; edited by Meg Mateo Ilasco ; foreword by Grace Bonney.

    p. cm.

  Includes index.

  ISBN 978-1-4521-0720-2

  1. Blogs. 2. Web site development—Amateurs' manuals. 3. Blogs—Economic aspects. 4. Blogs—Social aspects. 5. Marketing—Blogs. I. Ilasco, Meg Mateo. II. Title. III. Title: Blog, incorporated.

  TK5105.8884.C46 2012

  006.7'52—dc23

                                                2011042181

Manufactured in China

Designed by Meg Mateo Ilasco

10 9 8 7 6 5 4 3 2 1

Chronicle Books LLC

680 Second Street

San Francisco, California 94107

www.chroniclebooks.com

To my amazing blog readers,

Whether you've been reading since the beginning or just today, thank you for your dedication, encouragement, and for following along on this journey. You've given me a world of support and community I never knew existed.

Contents

Foreword

IN 2010, I PITCHED THE IDEA OF A "BLOGGING ETHICS" PANEL TO A POPULAR DESIGN CONFERENCE. When I told some of my friends, who were bloggers like me, they seemed to think I was crazy. "No one will want to hear about that" and "boring!" were common responses. Since I had been blogging for over six years and had learned so much about good (and bad) blogging practices, I wanted to have a serious discussion with members of our blogging community about the ethical issues we faced. My goal was to create an open dialogue where we could learn, improve our relationships with each other, and inspire collaboration. I was nervous about attendance, but a year later at the conference, our room was packed with more than 150 people. I looked at my panel mates, who included Joy Cho, with a huge smile. The ensuing discussion was *far* from boring, and my fellow bloggers once again surprised and impressed me with their excitement about a subject that allowed us to learn from and grow with each other.

However, this wasn't always the case. Back in 2004 when I started blogging, the phrase "Wild West" was used to describe our community on a regular basis. Those of us who were blogging about design knew little about what

> { . . . while everyone wants to know the secret to blogging success, the common denominator is to have a genuine and passionate voice that readers can connect with. }

were considered good blogging practices, and tended to have a "fly by the seat of our pants" mentality when it came to content, promotion, and turning our sites into real businesses. I distinctly remember other design bloggers asking me what the "rules" were and thinking, "Wow, I don't know if there *are* any." Thankfully, the blogging community has grown by leaps and bounds since then, and we've started to pay more attention to how we can be a more responsible form of media as well as build successful blogs and relationships with each other.

I never dreamed that I could start a site that would become my full-time job, and I'm so excited to see that being a full-time blogger is now an option for a new generation of writers, artists, and makers. When I started, I was happy just to have a place to share my thoughts, but in today's blogging world, the sky is the limit. I've been overjoyed to watch some of my blogging colleagues go on to open stores, write books, and host television programs based on the success of their Web sites. And while everyone wants to know the secret to blogging success, the common denominator is to have a genuine and passionate voice that readers can connect with.

I've been fortunate to call Joy one of my closest blogging friends over the past seven years, and she is in a unique position to share her vast knowledge about blogging. Her blog, Oh Joy!, has been the gold standard for lifestyle bloggers since she first started blogging in 2005. Her commitment to quality over quantity and dedication to maintaining a consistent voice rather than focusing on turning a quick profit has built her a loyal following. Whether you've been blogging for years or are just about to hit "Publish" on your first post, you can trust the advice you'll find in this book.

At its core, blogging is about having a safe place to share your voice and finding a community that cares about and connects with your interests. A handbook like this—full of advice from those who have already navigated the world of blogging—is one of the easiest ways to ensure that you develop and stay true to your core blogging goals and values. I hope that everyone reading this is inspired to speak their mind, join the blogging community, and work together with us to foster an ongoing spirit of excitement, collaboration, and inspiration.

Grace Bonney
DESIGN*SPONGE

Introduction

BACK IN 2001, WHEN A CO-WORKER TOLD ME ABOUT HER BLOG, I HAD NO IDEA WHAT IT WAS OR WHY ANYONE WOULD WANT ONE. **Blogging** gave me visions of Doogie Howser logging electronic diary entries of his adventures as a teen medical genius. I think a lot of people feel the same way, but I—and much of the world—have certainly come a long way in the past decade.

I have been a blogger since 2005: I was newly engaged, had just moved from New York to Philadelphia, and was looking for a new design job all at the same time. A friend of mine who maintained a blog as a creative outlet from her finance job suggested that I start one to chronicle this very transitional period in my life. At first I brushed it off, but I soon realized that I was in no position not to try it. In retrospect, starting a blog was one of the best decisions I've ever made. Although my blog, Oh Joy!, started off in a personal vein and was initially read by only a handful of friends, the site eventually evolved into a design-focused place where I share with tens of thousands of daily readers the projects I'm working on and the things that inspire my work. And I've gotten so much in return. My blog attracted buyers to my stationery line, raised my standing in the press (my blog was named one of *Time* magazine's top design sites in 2008), helped me to gain more dream clients for my design business, and even gave me the opportunity to write this book.

Even though blogs originated as a cyber version of the traditional personal diary, they have become a cultural force with the capacity to attract customers, create communities, and launch full-fledged careers. Bloggers serve as tour guides of their specific interests, passions, or skills, taking their readers on a journey through images, text, video, and interactive conversation. Through blogs, politicians, celebrities, Fortune 500 companies, and regular folks (like you and me) have an interactive platform to connect with fans, customers, and anyone who wants a deeper look into what inspires them. Thanks to how easy it is to start a blog, you can share your point of view with the potentially millions of Internet users out there craving inspiration, entertainment, or engagement with others. Whatever your talent, voice, or perspective is, a blog can offer you a sounding board: an instant audience that can give you feedback, advice, or support on your topic of choice. Success won't happen overnight. But if you dedicate your time and creativity to your blog, I guarantee that it will give you a sense of community you've never known before.

I clearly believe in the power of blogs. And since you're holding this book, you probably think there's something to them, too. This book may inspire you to launch your own blog or take an existing one to the next level. I wish I had a book like this when I started my blog. So here I've pulled together all the lessons I've learned, including those I discovered through my own blog and business, those I obtained by meeting fellow bloggers, and those I gleaned by following hundreds of other blogs along the way.

In *Blog, Inc.* I'll break down what makes a blog successful; how to create unique content, attract readers, and monetize; and show you how to blog to your best potential. I've also included interviews with fifteen bloggers (and a few businesses that work regularly with bloggers) whose focus ranges from fashion and cooking to weddings to art and design. Some blog as a hobby in addition to their 9-to-5 jobs, some juggle blogging with full-time parenting, some use blogs to market their business, and others consider themselves professional full-time bloggers. One thing that all the bloggers profiled here have in common: blogging has changed their lives.

The value of the creative outlet, community, career opportunities, and friendships my blog has brought me over the years is immeasurable. My blog took me on a path I never knew existed. I never actually ended up taking a design job I so actively sought at the time. The enthusiastic response to my design work from readers, and the clients that found me through my blog, motivated me to launch my own freelance design business, which eventually led to my developing a product line, writing and blogging for other publications, becoming an author, and consulting for other small creative businesses.

So whether you'd like to start a blog as a creative endeavor or to help market your business, share your talents, or connect with others, there's no reason not to start a blog today. It's time to put yourself out there, because you never know what amazing things will come your way.

{ INTRODUCTION *to* BLOGGING }

Whenever I talk to friends or clients who are struggling to figure out the next phase of their life or career, I always encourage them to start a blog. Maybe you're burnt out from your tedious 40-hour workweek and want to pursue your hobby of baking miniature pies full time. Or maybe you're a filmmaker and want to start offering tutorials on how the average person can create short films. A blog can be whatever you want it to be—a diary, a visual essay, an editorial space, a place for discussion and debate, or a scrapbook of inspiration. More than anything, a blog is a great way to get your ideas out into the world and see what people have to say in response. You could receive the feedback and kick in the pants you need to launch your new pie company or begin teaching film classes at your local college. In this chapter, I'll explain why you should blog, the types of blogs you could potentially have, and— the best part—how to get it all started.

BLOG *Basics*

A truncation of the term *Web log*, a *blog* is an interactive Web site that delivers regular content to its readers. Whether it's run by one person or multiple people, a blog is essentially a dynamic and ever-changing Web site that grows with every entry, or "post," that's created. Blogs are typically formatted like a newsfeed: the newest content appears at the top of the site, with the older posts descending below in reverse chronological order. The word *blog* has been adapted in other ways. It is used not only to describe a type

> { Blogging gives you a way to continually grab readers' attention with new posts and fresh doses of information. }

of site, but also the people who contribute to it ("Holy smokes—there's that fashion *blogger* I love"), the world pertaining to it ("I'm reading this awesome book that's giving me a crash course on the *blogosphere*"), and the process of doing it ("I'll be there in a minute; I'm *blogging* right now").

Blogging gives you a way to continually grab readers' attention with new posts and fresh doses of information. Unlike a book or print magazine, which gives consumers information in a single serving, a blog offers readers ongoing free content. They can read your posts whenever they want. Thanks to how quickly material can be posted, blogs often publish breaking news before traditional print and television media. Fashion blogs can post a designer's new fall collection as soon as photos are released, whereas a magazine will need to wait until the next issue goes to print. Many news and celebrity gossip stories show up on blogs before they are filmed and broadcast on live TV.

In an increasingly wired society, more and more of the mainstream population are browsing the Internet every day and spending at least part of that time reading blogs. What does that mean for you? It means that your possible audience is pretty big—including the billions of people in the world who currently use the Internet.

WHY *Blog?*

With literally hundreds of millions of public blogs in existence, you may be asking yourself, "Why should I add one more?" Because you have something unique to say, too! Someone out there is interested in your home renovation project because they're also working on their home, or is so touched by the crafts you're making to raise funds for your favorite charity that it inspires them to help others as well. Below are some of the main reasons to blog and how it can enrich your life, both personally and professionally.

№ 1 *Passion*

Maybe you're a nut for interior design and find yourself constantly rearranging your living room furniture. Or you love planning parties and are always looking for new ways to wow the guests at your next bash. Whatever your hobby or passion, blogging offers you a place to record your finds and ideas and share them with future Martha Stewarts and Candice Olsons.

№ 2 *Community*

Whether you're launching a new bakery or have just become a new mom, blogging can capture the attention of the community of people who share your interests, can offer you feedback, and become the friends you never knew you could have. Readers may also find your life story encouraging and inspiring as they go through the same joys or challenges in their own lives.

№ 3 *Marketing*

Online marketing is essential for every business today, and blogging is one of the best ways to give current and potential customers a peek into what makes your business tick. Not only will customers love giving suggestions regarding your bookstore's next author of the month, but they tend to be more loyal when they feel like they're getting access to the brain behind the business.

№ 4 *Share Talents*

Wedding photographer, carpenter, Pilates instructor—whatever your skills may be, if you blog to showcase your best work, it's likely that more clients will come your way. Remember, any reader is a potential client or customer!

№ 5 *Income*

While success may not come overnight, blogging has the potential to be a moneymaking venture. There are bloggers, including the ones profiled in this book, who make part or all of their income through their blog. With lots of hard work, patience, a unique point of view, and a go-getter attitude, you could be one of them, too. But be warned: profit should not be your main motivation for blogging. Your love for a particular topic and passion for sharing it with others will naturally produce a more interesting site. And that will, in turn, offer the potential for it to be a sustainable venture on its own.

A PAINTER AND MUSICIAN, Joel Henriques was waiting tables and bartending at Portland restaurants to supplement his and his wife's income. When their twins (a boy and girl) were born, he quit his restaurant duties and found he had less time to pursue his musical and artistic hobbies once he transitioned into full-time dad mode. Yet he became increasingly fascinated with watching his kids play. Despite the fancy wooden teething rings and toys that he and his wife had purchased, the babies were surprisingly drawn to their drool bibs. Their love of the texture and material in these simple objects inspired Joel to start making his own toys for them. These toys, including modern stuffed animals and a wooden elephant puzzle, sparked the interest of his art buyers and family members, so he began a blog, Made by Joel, to keep track of his creations. Made by Joel includes craft projects that parents, educators, and children can make, encouraging creativity and play and inspiring families to spend more quality time together. Joel has since collaborated with Disney, published a book based on his blog, and entered into a toy licensing partnership.

Who reads your blog, and why do you think they enjoy it?

I have a lot of parents, caregivers, teachers, and libraries that want to find something fun to do with their kids or the kids they teach. My readers are worldwide, from parents in the United States to preschool teachers in France. People love that the projects are modern and kid-friendly yet very easy for an adult without any craft skills to do with the children.

Another type of reader I didn't expect, but am thrilled to have, includes charity organizations, which ask if they can use my stuffed toy patterns to make toys and donate to children in need. Also, I always grant permission to use our projects as a learning aid. I want to make it easy for people or schools to find simple ways to enrich their children's art education. I'm able to provide

- - - - - →

a lot of free resources—making it easier for people to find creative projects, thereby filling the need for art that isn't supported in all schools. I have such a loyal following because of this, and I think people see that I'm not in it just for the money, but that I truly love helping kids foster their creativity.

What types of projects do you feature?

A lot of the projects I feature are based on things I think my kids will like or things that they thought of and I expanded on. For example, one day they were in the yard playing with flowers, and my son stacked a bunch of azaleas together in such a way that it looked like a flamenco dress. So we put it on a stand and turned it into a doll. I turned that into a project on my blog, which readers loved because they could easily duplicate it with materials they had at home or in their backyard. I always think about how I can make it easy for others to create the projects, too. Once I realized that I could upload higher-resolution pieces, like PDF templates, that opened up a whole other world of sharing, including coloring sheets and play sets. In addition to the projects, I also feature kids' music, other artists, the charities that are using our kits to help others, and moments from our lives with our kids. In the end, all the content is centered on the art and giving kids projects to play with.

What types of projects or opportunities have come from your blog?

My blog got its first big boost in traffic after BloesemKids posted about me. She has this "Mommy Stories" column, and I was the first daddy story featured in it. After that, I started getting more traffic and was approached by companies to work on projects together. I had said in an interview that someday I'd like to make my own book about crafts with simple, modern designs, and a couple of weeks later, I got approached by Shambala Books (distributed by Random House) to see if I'd want to publish my book with them. I wrote the book *Made to Play!* over the course of six months, and it was released in 2011. I now produce my elephant puzzle and other wooden toys with a company in London that approached me with the idea of licensing my toys under the Made by Joel brand. Finally, I've created a bunch of craft projects for various magazines in Europe, for Cheerios, and for Disney's *FamilyFun* magazine and have started a company to produce some of my own toys. I also got to fly to New York to be a guest on *The Martha Stewart Show*, which was an amazing experience.

Do you use any other social media tools to interact with your readers?

Yes, I have a lot of community interaction and feedback on my Facebook fan page. I think of the Web site as the "glossy magazine" and Facebook as a more personal part of the site. There's quite an active community there. I ask questions like "What do your kids like to play with in the backyard?" and I learn a lot from readers' suggestions. Not only are they giving me great ideas for other activities with kids, but they are also giving me feedback on the projects I provide and how they've changed them to suit their needs. It's like having a virtual playdate!

Do you have any concerns about featuring your kids on your blog?

Everyone in my family is really into art and really excited about the growth of the blog. My wife and I never had any concerns about featuring our kids, but we'll have certain limitations, like we don't use their names very often, or we don't put them in some of the YouTube videos I'll make. We do what feels comfortable.

How has your role as a daddy blogger helped encourage other dads to play a more active part in their children's learning and play?

I get a lot of e-mails from other dads who are happy to have found my site and enjoy the types of projects I provide. But most of my e-mails are from moms, who tell me about the projects their husbands did and how they are using my ideas to play with their kids more. Even if the projects aren't things they've done before, they are easy to do. Also, the projects I devise are a bit on the masculine side for the crafting world, in that they might require parents to break out their tool kit or use wire or wood, which are materials that dads usually like. It's fun to hear how everyone in the family bonds over the creation of these toys and projects. It's really fun to have a job that involves my kids and my family. I feel really lucky to be doing this as my job.

TYPES of BLOGS

You've got the itch to start a blog, so now it's time to figure out where yours will find its home in the blogosphere. There is no wrong way to go about it, but it helps to start with a certain focus on what you'll be sharing with the world. What are your interests and passions, and what topics seem like the most fun for you to share with others? What's something you've always been interested in but haven't had the chance to tackle yet? Is there a topic you love but have a hard time finding content about online? Blogs can be just one kind or incorporate different types, here's a look at five main variations of blogs you could establish.

PERSONAL

Maybe you've just changed jobs, had a new baby, or are embarking on a year-long trip around the world. A personal blog can highlight whatever aspect of your life you choose to share with others. You could document a big life change or focus on the joys of the everyday as a way to keep friends and family, near and far, abreast of personal happenings. Whatever your reason for starting one, a personal blog can be a great way to record your life's journey with words and photos. It can be so rewarding to look back on your

{ Whatever your reason for starting one, a personal blog can be a great way to record your life's journey with words and photos. }

growing baby bump or the miles you logged training for a marathon and see how much you've changed or accomplished since you started. While you may hesitate at the idea of allowing just anyone to get a glimpse into your personal life, many find that the community of support and interaction they build with others makes it very worthwhile. If it makes you more at ease, you can always password-protect your blog in the beginning, until you feel more comfortable letting it be a public place for all to see.

TOPICAL

A topical blog showcases your interests, passions, and hobbies. And keep in mind that you don't have to choose just one topic. If you're interested in both gardening and cooking, you could have a blog that chronicles both interests independently, but also consider creating posts that merge them together. For example, you could post a recipe with images of a dish prepared with veggies picked straight from your backyard garden. A blog that focuses on your passions is likely to attract readers who have similar interests and hobbies, and help you connect with others as well. Many times we say we'll embark on a new hobby or make time for a new creative outlet that we've always dreamed of diving into, but then other parts of our lives take over and those aspirations get put on the back burner. A blog gives you a perfect excuse to not only immerse yourself in this always-talked-about pursuit, but pushes you to stay on top of it once you're giving updates for anyone to read. It makes you accountable and encourages you to keep those ideas flowing once readers look forward to reading your posts and inspirations.

TALENT

Let's say you're a budding watercolor artist or a hairstylist. A blog can serve as an up-to-the-minute portfolio of your recent personal and professional work. Maybe you've been working on a drawing a day, or you recently helped style coifs for a catalog shoot. Even if you're an emerging artist who hasn't found your specific style yet, a blog can serve as a virtual sketchbook, allowing you to practice your photography or mixed-media sculptures and post them for others to see and offer feedback. Keeping a blog that showcases your work not only helps you to connect with other talented folks in your field, but also can be a great marketing tool to reach potential customers and clients.

BEHIND-THE-SCENES NEWS

These days, some of the most successful businesses are those that know how to interact with their customers on a more personal level. Especially since so many companies exist virtually these days, a blog can help a business, big or small, interact with customers from all over the world. A stay-at-home mom from Indiana can give her Etsy store customers in other cities shop updates and a glimpse into her process for making organic soaps. For the same reasons that documentary TV shows or movies pull you in, consumers love having a sense of involvement or getting a behind-the-scenes picture of their favorite personalities and brands. Maybe you're getting ready to open the doors to the flower shop of your dreams, or you've been running your family's thirty-year-old furniture business, and it needs a fresh boost.

COMMUNITY/COLLABORATIVE

If you have friends or colleagues who share similar interests, hobbies, or skills, why not join forces and create something together? You and a long-distance friend can track your foodie adventures in two different cities, or you and some fellow alumni can collaborate on a blog that tracks your post-graduate paths. In a collaborative blog, two or more people contribute to the content of a site. It's a great way to get different perspectives on a topic and offer more content than you could otherwise create on your own—this is ideal if the thought of maintaining a blog seems daunting. Just keep in mind that the responsibilities here should also be shared. It helps to plan ahead of time who will post on what days and how often, as well as decide whose role it will be to review comments or respond to reader e-mails.

While these are the main types of blogs, you don't have to choose just one. A good thing about blogging is that it's an ever-changing format that can evolve with you as you grow. For example, you can decide as you go to blend a bit of your personal life with details on your craft ideas and projects. Many blogs these days include a combination of things—like one's talent and personal life—so as long as your point of view stays consistent, readers often enjoy the mix.

ANATOMY of a BLOG

Blogs can range from the super-basic to the complex, but at the heart of every blog are certain universal functions and features. The chapters to come will delve into these topics in more detail, but to get you up to speed on the lingo, here's a look at the most common elements of a blog.

URL (uniform resource locator). The specific address on the Internet that readers will type to find your daily musings.

Banner. Like the cover of a magazine, your banner is the first thing readers will see when visiting your blog. A well-considered header is a blog must. Be sure it grabs a reader's attention and includes your blog's name as well as some graphics or imagery that hint at your blog's content. If you're going to spend any money at all on your blog, this might be the place to do it.

Title. Short and sweet, witty, poignant, or funny, the title of a post gives readers an introduction to what they'll be seeing or reading in your blog.

Post. The meat of your site will be the entries, or posts, you generate, preferably on a regular basis. This is where you'll tell a story through images, text, video, or a combination of these elements.

Post Date. This tells a reader the date and time of a post as a reference for when the information was posted.

Permalink. This is the unique URL of a blog post. This address is helpful when you want to link back to an old post that's no longer on your front page, or if other bloggers want to reference one of your posts.

Hyperlink. Usually appearing in a different color or as underlined text, a hyperlink indicates to readers that the text can be clicked on and will take them to another Web page. You'll use hyperlinks when you want to credit an image source, tell readers where to buy something you blogged about, link to a post that you love on another blog, or reference a past post in your own archive.

Comments. Comments on your blog let you interact with your readers and give you insight into which content your readers enjoy the most, or least.

Trackback. A trackback shows you when another blogger loves your content enough to link to your post on his or her blog. So if you enable trackbacks, your blog will list all the other places where one of your posts is being reposted or mentioned.

Categories. Like file folders, categories allow you to file a post in a particular section in case readers want to see every post related to a topic you cover. As you generate new posts, you can place each into a category (e.g., "Things for My Home" or "Kitchen Tools").

Tags. Tags serve as complements to categories and refine them further. In addition to placing a post in a general category, you can tag it using specific keywords. For example, if you have a category about interiors, you can tag a post with the keywords *bedroom* or *wallpaper* to more clearly define the various topics in that post. Or if you have a chocolate category on your blog, tags may include *truffles*, *cupcakes*, or *frosting* to narrow the type of chocolate even further.

Archives. The archives are a log of all your posts and are usually organized by month, listed from the current month backward.

RSS Feed. RSS, or really simple syndication, allows readers to subscribe to all the blogs they like and view them in one place without having to visit each site independently or directly. Many Web browsers offer a way to subscribe to blog feeds, or you can provide a link to your site's RSS so that readers can subscribe to your feed. Depending on your reader's subscription method, your blog feed may show up in their Internet browser, e-mail inbox, or a specified reader account, like Google Reader.

Blogroll. Usually placed in the side column of your blog, a blogroll is a list of the blogs that you enjoy and recommend, allowing you to show support for other bloggers.

Widgets. A widget is an application that can be installed in your blog to enhance it, like a search box field or a box that shows your Twitter feed. Widgets should be installed only if they are helpful to your site or relevant to your content, as they take up space and increase load time.

Sponsor Ads. When your readership is large enough to be enticing to potential advertisers, you may choose to offer sponsor ads. Usually consisting of still jpegs or animated gifs, these ads can be in a range of sizes and can appear either in your side column, in between posts, or at the header or footer of your blog.

ONE DAY, while designing textile patterns for a client, freelance graphic designer Lauren Willhite found herself unmotivated and uninspired. She needed to come up with interesting color combinations for the project but could not find reliable color resources online. So she started her blog, Color Collective, in 2010 as an inspirational tool for herself, hoping that other designers would find the blog useful as well. Along with posting various images from the Internet that inspire her, Lauren pulls five colors from each image and joins them together as swatches to show the color palette. Now, creatives of all kinds—even design heavyweights like handbag designer Rebecca Minkoff and J.Crew creative director Jenna Lyons—use her blog for color inspiration when dreaming up new projects and collections.

? *What types of images do you post and pull color inspiration from?*

I pull any image that inspires me, including ones based on art and design, interiors, and fashion images. I studied photography in high school before majoring in graphic design in college, so it's important to me that all of the images are beautifully photographed.

? *How do readers use your color combinations for their work or as inspiration?*

Many quilters and knitters have e-mailed me, saying that they print out my posts and take them to the fabric or yarn store when picking out their materials. I have also received e-mails from brides-to-be who are picking out wedding colors. Interior designers, surface designers, graphic designers, and clothing designers have expressed appreciation for Color Collective, as they use the palettes in their own design work. I am humbled to have been told by Rebecca Minkoff and Jenna Lyons personally that they use my blog for

-----→

color inspiration! One benefit of having a color blog is that it is not confined to one specific area—color palettes are used in so many different fields. I also started a Color Collective Flickr group so that people could show their own creations that were inspired by my posts.

As a newbie, how did you become more active in the blog community?

I sent out personalized e-mails to my favorite bloggers to let them know about my blog in case they had any interest in checking it out. I also left a lot of comments on other people's blogs hoping that people would track back to mine. Becoming an intern for Chelsea Fuss's blog Frolic! was extremely helpful, too. I started interning with Chelsea in March 2010, just a few months after starting Color Collective. I helped her out in many areas, from researching and coming up with new blog posts to prop shopping and lending an extra hand styling photo shoots. In return, Chelsea was willing to meet with me weekly to discuss and answer any questions I had about blogging. Chelsea got me started on Twitter and Facebook and gave me tips on how to broaden my circle of blogging friends and join other social networks. I would have had no idea about how to start asking for sponsors without Chelsea's help! I also noticed that my eye for curating images online became stronger after the three-month internship. Chelsea has a beautiful sense of style, and I found that I became more selective about what I posted on my own blog.

When did you start getting sponsors, and how did you go about starting your ad program?

I started my sponsor program about seven months after I began the blog. At the time I was getting around 600 visitors per day. I created a sponsor information sheet that has my stats, press, and rates, and just tried to spread the word through Twitter, Facebook, and, of course, the blog itself. I used to wait for people to approach me about becoming a sponsor, but every now and then when I see a shop or blog that I think would be a great fit for Color Collective, I will send them an e-mail with my sponsor information sheet.

? *Have any special opportunities come from starting your blog?*

Jen Ford, fashion news director at *Lucky* magazine, sent me an e-mail about eight months after I started Color Collective. She said that the *Lucky* office was impressed with my blog, and after an office vote, they wanted to feature my idea in the magazine! In *Lucky*'s February 2011 issue, Color Collective was mentioned in the Editor's Notes. Then, in the following four issues (March through June), I chose a piece of artwork and pulled a color palette made up of five colors from each image. The *Lucky* team would then find a shoppable outfit to match the style and colors of the artwork. I worked together with the editors to come up with a paragraph to complete each page. In February 2011, I was honored to join the *Lucky* FABB [Fashion and Beauty Blogger] Conference in New York City. I had the chance to meet fellow fashion and beauty bloggers, and I learned so much about social networking and blogging from speakers such as Rich Tong, Tumblr's fashion director; Tory Burch, a fashion designer; and Joan Rivers, the comedian.

? *What types of collaborations have you had with other blogs?*

Starting Color Collective opened up opportunities to collaborate with other bloggers. Design*Sponge has always been a favorite, so I was delighted when Grace Bonney asked me to do a week of guest posts in June 2010. For the posts, I found images of interiors that inspired me and pulled color palettes accompanied by paint names and Pantone numbers. After the series, Grace asked me to become a regular contributor with my own weekly column. The column is called "Make It Yours": I pick out my favorite, colorful interiors from her "Sneak Peek" archives, pull color palettes from two different rooms, find paint names and Pantone numbers to match the colors, and then create a collage of five or six products that have a similar style to the rooms.

I also contribute to another of my daily reads, Design for Mankind, as a weekly contributor. The column is called "Color Mankind": I pick an image that fits the Design for Mankind aesthetic and create a color palette to go with the image. I feel very lucky to have a chance to work with these bloggers I admire.

{ FINDING YOUR VOICE *and* NICHE }

There's always room for something new and exciting in the blogo-sphere, so what will you add to the dialogue? The possibilities are endless. That itch to start something new or share your perspective is often the driving force behind any blogger's place on the Web. But how do you make your blog sound, feel, and look like an exten-sion of yourself? Many successful bloggers find that developing a vision and voice that they can stay true to and that makes them stand out keeps their readers coming back for more. In this chapter, I'll help you find your blog's personality, come up with a distinctive name, hone your writing style, and figure out just how to produce content for your blog that's uniquely you.

YOUR BLOG'S PERSONALITY *and* NICHE

When readers come to your blog, they should immediately get a sense of your personality and niche. Do you want something quirky, funny, poetic, or serious? Even if you have no intention of ever earning income off of this site (or especially if you plan to), from Day One you'll want to give some thought to what will make your blog special.

The motivation for starting your blog may stem from admiring blogs that you can't get enough of. Maybe you think, "Oh, I'd love to have a site just like theirs!" or "That's the kind of thing I want to blog about!" It's great to look at other blogs you enjoy for inspiration, but remember that you need to

> It's great to look at other blogs you enjoy for inspiration, but remember that you need to bring your own unique spin to your blog.

bring your own unique spin to your blog. When figuring out what the content of your site should be and how you could convey information in your own unique way, it's helpful to ask yourself the following questions:

Why are you blogging? Is it a hobby or personal outlet? A marketing tool for your business? Something you see as a potential career? Knowing the purpose of your blog will help you to steer your tone and focus toward your goal—whether it's connecting with other artisanal cheese enthusiasts, reaching customers who love your handmade quilts, or interacting with other stay-at-home moms.

Who is your target audience? Are they mostly female or male? What age range do they fall into? Are they city dwellers or country folks? Do they live abroad? Your audience may end up being different from who you imagine them to be now, but it's a good idea to target the type of person who would be interested in the topics you're planning to cover. If you're a typographer and want to reach others in the graphic design community (or potential clients) with your found-type blog, your images and tone should be very visual and graphic, and you should post a variety of images to inspire others with the typography that you both create and find.

What blogs have content similar to yours? After you come up with some ideas about what you'll blog about, it's helpful to check to see what blogs out there already have similar content. That way you can avoid an over-saturated category or see what's missing from the existing perspectives to make sure that yours fills a void or offers a new take on your subject. For example, among the many female-focused wedding blogs out there, the Well Groomed blog is a place where men's style meets matrimony to give grooms a site to seek ideas for groomsmen gifts as well as outfits for their big day.

Why should someone read your blog? What makes it unique? The best blogs are ones that add their own unique twist or style to a topic. What ideas do you have that will make yours different? Do you end every post with a haiku, or are all your images purposely black-and-white? A street-style blog may not be totally new these days, but if you include stylish locals seen with their adorable (and equally fashionable) pooches, it just may be a fun spin on street style that's unique to you and your love of animals and fashion trends.

YOUR *Blog's* AESTHETIC

Regardless of whether your blog chronicles what you ate for breakfast, the newest indie filmmaker, or your favorite interiors, you must establish a consistent look and tone throughout the blog that makes it stylistically feel like you—the font and type styles used, colorways, and types of imagery. Erica Domesek's chic craft blog, P.S. – I Made This…, gives first-time readers a clue to its crafty yet glam nature with its handwritten header and step-by-step layouts that look like pages pulled from an inspirational sketchbook. To help figure out the look of your blog, start by collecting images and text from

{ . . . you must establish a consistent look and tone throughout the blog that makes it stylistically feel like you . . . }

magazines and the Internet that inspire you, and ties to the content you plan to post. Put all of these elements together in a "mood board" by taping them on a wall or pinning them to a bulletin board. When you take a step back and look at the collection of references you've put together, you'll start to see what your aesthetic really is. You may even notice some outliers that don't fit with the dominant style you've pulled together. This is when you'll learn to start editing your vision to make it more focused. All of these components brought together will create a visual guide for you to take your cue from as you move forward with your blog's aesthetic.

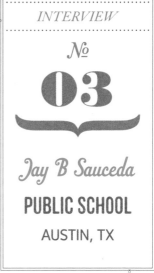

Jay B Sauceda

PUBLIC SCHOOL

AUSTIN, TX

WHEN YOU ENVISION A GROUP of guys gathered together under one roof, a college frat house might come to mind. In contrast, the guys of Public School (Casey Dunn, Cody Haltom, Jay B Sauceda, Justin Cox, Matthew Genitempo, Shaun Lind, and Will Bryant) are a collective of photographers, illustrators, and designers who work together in one space and run one pretty cool blog. Before the collective, they were working individually at home or bouncing around coffee shops. Through their mutual friendships, the group manifested with a joint vision to create great work both individually and collaboratively under the Public School brand. They all contribute to the Public School blog, which serves to highlight their work, while sharing things they find interesting in art, design, science, technology, or music. Through their joint work and blog, these non-frat boys show how they believe in the value of working together to create something stronger and more diverse than they otherwise could separately on their own.

? *What made you decide to start a collaborative blog?*

Cody and I had kicked around the idea of starting a blog because we noticed a lot of design- and art-oriented Web sites were showing other people's work, not just their own. We found that when reading blogs, people respond to your taste in addition to the work you can produce. We wanted people to come to our site because they like our content, and then maybe they'd learn about our own work, too. So we decided collectively to start our group blog, and created the name, Public School, with the idea of sharing lots of different ideas, and then named our shared studio and collective space after it.

? *How did you decide on the type of content for the blog?*

When we started it in 2008, everyone had varying tastes based on what their professions were. I tend to read more tech, science, furniture, and lifestyle blogs, whereas Cody, in comparison, is more into pop culture and design. I'm

- - - - - ->

not great at finding highbrow art, whereas Will is really good at that. Initially, we didn't blog as much because we were trying to be solely focused on art and design topics and found that it was hard to blog only on those topics. Then we decided to open it up to a more lifestyle-based blog with a heavy art and design focus, because it made it easier for all seven of us to contribute.

? *How do you decide how often to post, and what gets posted? Is there a set schedule or plan?*

At this point, we've figured out what our varying tastes are and what types of things each of us will post. We don't edit each other, because our readership is into the different things that each of us like. We like that it's a mix of things from all of us. It's cool for me to read our blog, too, since I'm interested to see what will be blogged about by the other guys, and I don't always know what's going to show up.

As for a schedule, we've grown into the habit of blogging less in the summer because traffic is usually lower due to readers being on vacation more. But in the fall or spring, we'll post about four or five times a day. We don't require everyone to post a certain amount, because it's easier for some of us to blog, and there are some who are more interested in it. Will and I try and make it a point to post once or twice a day; we're the most consistent. Because we're all blogging while also trying to do our client work, everyone picks up the slack when one person is busy and can't blog as much during that time.

? *What's the best part of having a collaborative blog?*

I think it serves the purpose that we intended in that it's gotten our name out there more than we could have done individually. When you work for yourself, you have to be all over the place all at once to get your work noticed. Our work propagates pretty easily and gets spread around through our blog. It drives me to create more work, and I look forward to posting when I know our readers will be interested in it. The whole idea of Public School was that it wasn't going to be about one type of work or attract one type of reader or client. I like that we attract a variety of aesthetics and readers through our varied members' interests.

? *How has your blog helped to increase awareness about the creative community in Austin?*

Even though the Austin scene is still relatively small compared to bigger cities in the country, our blog has served to show that there are world-class photographers, illustrators, and all kinds of artists here. We're all proud to be living here and glad that we don't have to live in a major West Coast or East Coast city to do what we do. That's the beauty of the Internet—the ability to create your world and show your work in front of thousands of people and create conversations with people from all over.

PARTNERS IN CRIME

You might be surprised to find that behind many a blogger there's a significant other or supportive family member in the background, helping to make the blog bigger, better, and more dynamic. You can't do everything, so if someone near and dear to you has a special skill or talent, why not call upon them to help you out with your newfound hobby? Kirsten Grove seeks her cousin Evan Earwicker's technical and programming skills to make her popular Simply Grove blog more functional as her site grows. Emily Schuman from Cupcakes and Cashmere would be without a photographer to capture her daily clothing ensembles if it weren't for her husband, Geoffrey, who's learned to use a digital SLR to help record his wife's virtual chronicles. So if your loved one's got the magic touch with a camera or a technical mind that just doesn't come naturally to you, see if they'll contribute their talents to help you build the blog of your dreams.

NAMING *Your* BLOG

Like the title of a movie or book, the name of your blog sets the tone of it and should give readers an idea of what they are about to see. Choosing a name for your blog may seem overwhelming at first—and indeed, it's a crucial step, as you can't start a blog or reserve a domain name until you find that special moniker. The sooner you come up with a name, the sooner you can start blogging, and that's where all the fun begins! It can be tempting to start a blog on a whim, but don't hastily start posting under the first name that occurs to you. A little foresight—and some significant soul searching— will pay off in the end.

While your blog name doesn't need to clearly spell out your blog's content, it's often helpful if the name hints at your topic of choice. The blog Bakerella immediately tells readers that sweet baked goods are sure to be involved, while Lovely Package offers a fun play on words and alludes to the

> While your blog name doesn't need to clearly spell out your blog's content, it's often helpful if the name hints at your topic of choice.

site's focus on packaging design. If you haven't settled on a specific topic yet or you want your blog to encompass a few of your different interests, a play on words can be a good way to tell a bit about your blog without getting too literal or serious. Joanna Goddard's A Cup of Jo hints at her first name while also referencing that, like coffee, people might like to enjoy her site as a morning ritual. And Scanwiches merges two words together to indicate a blog that features cross sections of scanned sandwiches.

You'll also want to think about the potential growth of your blog. While you may be really into French cheeses now and want to have a blog name that reflects that love, could you see the potential to eventually expand into taste testing and blogging about other types of French foods? If so, then "The French Market" may be a little more encompassing of future topics than "Ma Vie en Fromage."

Simple names are great as long as they feel special as well. As much as your blog will certainly be cool, naming it "The Cool Blog" may make it hard to find when readers conduct an Internet search for your site. Think of ways you can make the name more specific, or better yet, turn that generic noun or adjective into a different or nonexistent version of a word, like the men's gadget blog The Awesomer. Also, blog names that have the potential to work themselves into recurring post titles can be fun, too. For example, the blog You Are My Fave includes the words *are my fave* in all its post titles, like "Rainbow Pops Are My Fave" and "Summer Watercolors Are My Fave."

When coming up with a blog name that includes uncommon words or word combinations, it helps to do the "friend test." Show friends the name you're pondering and see if they can pronounce it and remember how to spell it the next day. The same is true for lengthy names. Plus, nobody wants to type in a twenty-letter-long URL, so keep that in mind when something like "The Girl with the Green Rubber Boots and Yellow Hat" springs to mind as a potential name. Also, when using a social networking tool like Twitter, a drawn-out twitter handle based on your blog name may get in the way of what followers can say to you or about your blog, since Twitter only allows 140 characters for communicating a message. Because "word of mouse" is one of the best ways to grow your readership, an easy-to-remember name can help a reader remember your blog, making it easier for them to spread the word.

Since blog names are viewed as URLs, do one more test and take a look at the name when it's typed into a Web browser. All of a sudden the lack of spacing may make it much harder to figure out, or it could be read as something else completely. The blog "Fun Dynasty" may be read as "Fundy Nasty" when typed into a browser with no spacing. While that play on words may be part of your shtick, it's something worth testing out in case it's not.

Once you've settled on a name or have a list of your top five, search for these names on the Internet and make sure they're not already being used by someone else. Also, check the U.S. Patent and Trademark Office's Web site for any conflicts (see Resources). Be sure to steer clear of any names that belong to a company to avoid being slapped with a cease-and-desist order down the road and being forced to change your blog's name and URL after you've established a steady following. If the name is already being used by another business, pick something else. The same is true for a name that's really similar to an existing blog. If "The Crafty Girl" is already taken, making it "The Crafty Girl's Guide" is still too similar. It would be best to come up with an alternative name that won't raise any question of who is who. While the blogger may not have officially trademarked their name, it's better to be safe and avoid any brand confusion or conflict later on.

TAKING CARE OF BUSINESS

If you're creating a blog as an extension of your existing company, you'll want to capitalize on any brand recognition your business already has by keeping your blog name, voice, and look consistent. Sometimes, business owners see their blog as a chance to create something new. Stay consistent with the brand you've already built; otherwise a new name or look could alienate your current customers if it isn't obvious that the blog belongs to you. For example, if you own a gardening shop called "Green Thumb," the blog can simply be called "Green Thumb," too, or an offshoot like "Chronicles of the Green Thumb." Keep the logo and aesthetic similar so that your current and future customers understand that the blog is an extension of your shop and not a brand-new business altogether.

Joelle Hoverson

THE PURL BEE

NEW YORK, NY

A FORMER EDITOR at Martha Stewart Living Omnimedia and a freelance stylist, Joelle Hoverson had been a longtime knitter over the years. Her side hobby eventually spiraled into a full-on obsession, compelling Joelle to open a knitting shop in her favorite New York neighborhood, SoHo, in 2002. Joelle was later joined at Purl Soho by her two partners, Jennifer Hoverson Jahnke (in 2003) and Page Marchese Norman (in 2008). Purl Soho started as a modest 400-square-foot shop and eventually moved to a larger location, encompassing sewing and fabric supplies in addition to knitting materials. As their shop expanded, the women found they wanted to interact with their online customers more, to offer support and tips on the various projects their clients needed help with. So they started their blog, The Purl Bee, in 2006 to foster a conversation around craft projects and to serve as a virtual community for those who didn't have physical access to their store. Joelle admits that the blog is one of her favorite parts of the business—she loves the community it's created and the stories they are able to share through their DIY projects and posts.

? *Why did you decide to start your blog, The Purl Bee, as an extension of your shop?*

In 2006, we expanded from our tiny 400 square feet by renting another store down the street to hold fabric. We named it Purl Patchwork. At the time, I had heard about blogs—and had noticed that the whole craft blog world was such a vibrant community—but I wasn't savvy about them. In 2003, we launched our online store, PurlSoho.com. However, one of the things that frustrated me was that we weren't going to be able to talk to our customers online the way we do when they come into our physical store. We wanted to be able to offer suggestions, give tips, and help our online customers with their projects. So we thought that a blog would be a great way to talk to

-----→

them. The Purl Bee has ended up being an incredible force for our company and one of my favorite parts of the business. Now, we post at least twice a week and coordinate one of the posts with our Sunday night newsletter so that we always have a new project up on the blog when the e-mail newsletter goes out.

You create beautiful DIY sewing and craft projects on your blog. How do you come up with the projects you feature?

We make projects specifically for the blog. In addition to Page and me, we have a staff of three people at Purl Soho who also work on the blog and have their own columns. We hold weekly meetings to discuss our ideas about what we want to make. Typically everyone has their own area of expertise—one person does knitting and crochet, another person does the sewing, etc. Once we decide that something is a good fit, someone will take on the project. We're always trying to teach something to our customers. And when we can, we like to inspire them with something we have in the store—like a new tool or a material we just love. On average, it takes about six weeks from the time a concept is presented as an idea in our weekly meeting to the time it's finished and posted.

How do you weave products from the shop into those projects? Do you find that readers respond more to certain types of projects than others?

One of our most popular posts was a really simple flower made from embroidery thread using a flower loom that we were selling. We sold out of those things five times over, to the point where we couldn't get any more from the vendor. So there will be posts like that—simple, yet that create a lot of interest in a specific product. In contrast, we had a very involved story about binding and quilting. That story generated a lot of traffic because it was all about a very involved technique, but it did not generate a lot of specific sales. We really try to do a mix of both longer, drawn-out projects and some that you can do quickly in a couple of hours.

? *How has your blog helped grow your shop and customer base?*

It's helped our shop grow a lot. The blog does really well in the search engines because there is always new content, and it's packed full of information. I really believe that word of mouth is the best advertising, and our blog has increased our exposure on a level we could never have achieved with traditional advertising. People come in the store every day who have read the blog and want to buy supplies to make a recently featured project.

BEING *Authentic*

As every blogger interviewed in this book will tell you, it's so important to be true to yourself in the way you write, the images you post, and the type of content you share. Anything that feels forced and doesn't freely come out of you will make it hard for you to enjoy blogging regularly and to maintain it down the road. That doesn't mean that you have to share every moment of your life with your readers. Authenticity simply means writing in a voice that comes naturally to you, and posting things that you simply want to share with others—not what you *think* they want to see. I often receive e-mails from companies asking me to post about their products—sometimes in exchange for compensation. However, I never post about something (paid or not) if I wouldn't use or buy it myself. Do the same, and the readers who stick with you over time will learn to trust your taste and come to feel that what you blog about is genuine. (For more on sponsored content, see page 147.)

Blog WRITING AND VOICE

What do you want your blog to sound like? Like a comedic sitcom, a dramatic movie, a sonnet, an arthouse short film, a rock song? Some blogs are purely visual and only need a bit of text to credit the source of an image. But most blogs give readers at least a small dose of prose. Regardless of whether your blog concept involves a daily poem, recipes, narrative paragraphs, or a few short lines, make sure that whatever you write is instinctual and feels authentic to you. If you're based in France, you may choose to write in French or to write in both French and English so that your blog can reach those readers who aren't fluent in your native tongue. Your style of writing should reflect your point of view and the way you naturally write, think, and talk. If friends always remark on your sense of sarcasm and your hilarious one-liners, don't be afraid to bring that humor into your blog, like April Winchell does on her site Regretsy (see page 134). Or if your innate inclination is for witty prose, you could inject that into your posts. For example, Kelley Lilien of Mrs. Lilien uses rhyme to describe her '50s- and '60s-inspired lifestyle, making her sound like a glamorous modern-day Dr. Seuss. Whatever your tone, there's no need to feel locked into one voice right away. You're still taking your first steps as a blogger, so it's okay to let your voice evolve as you grow. Your natural tone is most likely what's running through your head when you're not even thinking about your blog, so always keep a notebook handy—you never know when a witty post title or a smart string of words will strike.

DEVELOPING A FICTIONAL PERSONA

Being authentic in your blog doesn't mean that your blog has to showcase exactly the way you live—in fact, some bloggers remain anonymous or write from a fictional persona to show another side of their personality. This can be a fun way to live vicariously through another character or personality that you've always wanted to portray. Blogging under the guise of a "hare-ess" socialite bunny, the anonymous writer, blogger, and illustrator of the fashion blog Fifi Lapin stays true to Fifi and all of her whims and idiosyncrasies (even in interviews for magazines like *Vogue* and *Elle*) as she posts illustrations of Fifi's daily couture ensembles and talks about her furry life of luxury.

LIFE DOESN'T ALWAYS have to be glamorous. It's the simple things—like family, friends, and neighborhood jaunts—that are actually the most memorable to Naomi Davis, whose blog, Rockstar Diaries, attracts more than one million page views per month and whose readers love witnessing how she celebrates the everyday. Naomi began her blog in 2007 while studying dance at Juilliard to keep family and friends updated on her life in New York as a dancer and newlywed. She subsequently moved to Washington, D.C., with her husband, Josh, and had their first child, Eleanor, a few years after. Blogging has become a creative outlet for Naomi that lets her show that having a family and being a young urbanite are not mutually exclusive. She documents everyday moments—like her daughter's giggle or her favorite burger joint—through high-contrast color photos created from a mix of the family's Polaroid, digital, and toy cameras. Because of Naomi's honest and charming demeanor (and her vivid photos to match), her daily posts can often generate as many as 200 reader comments, some simply appreciating her as a role model for young families everywhere. Whether musing about her bulldog, Kingsley; pizza feasts with her husband; weekend visits from her family; or the chubby belly of her baby girl, Naomi demonstrates the simple pleasures of life and shows that home is wherever your family is.

? *Where does the name Rockstar Diaries come from?*

To be honest, I named it Rockstar Diaries in the beginning just to be silly. If I'd known back in the day that it would stick and gain a bit of a following, I would have named it something different!

---->

What do you share with readers through your blog, and what do you make a conscious decision to leave off your blog?

Because my blog started with the intention of having just our friends and family read it, I've always blogged in a personal way and focused on my family's mundane moments: what we love to eat, weekend updates, thoughts on being a mother, and having a bulldog that we adore. It's about the simple things we love in life that make every day so special. There are definitely things I don't share. Sometimes readers forget that a blogger has a right to privacy as well. For example, I have chosen not to share my birth story on my blog, and many readers have expressed their disappointment in that. But my birth story is so personal and special to me, my husband, and, most important, my kids, and I'd like it to stay that way.

Did you ever feel pressured to change your blog or get less personal once your readership began to grow?

I've always enjoyed blogging on a personal level. The growth was very organic and gradual. I started receiving comments from strangers in my first couple of months of blogging, and then other blogs began to link to my site. When I realized there was a bigger audience, I still kept the content consistent, and I never felt drawn to change it. I want the blog to encapsulate a piece of me and my family. I don't think I'd enjoy it as much if I changed focus to another topic that I'm less passionate about.

Many of your family members make regular appearances on your blog. Did your husband or other relatives have any worries about privacy or putting their lives online for your readers to see?

I've asked family and friends who appear frequently on our blog if they're comfortable with it as our readership has grown, and so far no one has had a problem with it. But I've made an effort to leave off where family members live or what schools they are attending—only because when they're stopped by readers on the street or something, it catches them off guard. I don't mind when people approach us—I actually love meeting readers of my blog—but it's different with my sisters. I don't want them to feel weird at all as they go about their daily routines.

Did you have any issues or concerns with privacy, especially after Eleanor was born?

My husband and I go back and forth on this issue all the time, weighing the pros and cons of having a public blog. As of now, we are both comfortable with it. But I definitely feel as our kids grow older that this will change. I don't mind blogging about my life publicly, but as Eleanor grows and her personality forms, I imagine the blogging (photos specifically) of her will become less and less. I want her to be her own little person with her own little personality and not worry that her mother is tweeting and blogging about her every move.

What's your number one piece of advice to new bloggers?

Blog about what you are most interested in. Don't choose a topic because you think it will do better or reach more people. The content needs to be something that interests you and be unique to you. There are a handful of people who can make a full-time living blogging, and they work really hard to get there. But if you go into it for that reason alone, readers can sense that you're only in it for the stats or the money.

How has blogging helped you as a mother?

I gain so much inspiration from other mothers in the blogging world—it's such a special community to belong to. I look up to many of the mothers whose blogs I follow, and I think they've really impacted the way I want to raise our children. Blogging in general has helped me to keep up with journaling our lives in a sense, and I love that it holds me to documenting our life as a family. It keeps me accountable for writing down little landmarks or always having my camera handy to capture whatever Eleanor will do next. And I enjoy every minute of that.

Unique CONTENT

In addition to having a voice and point of view that expresses your personality, original content is essential for any blog. Because there is so much great information on the Internet, it's not uncommon to see the same images or stories on multiple blogs. While it's okay to blog about topics that other bloggers cover, too, you don't want your blog to consist primarily of things that readers have already seen elsewhere. Otherwise, they won't feel as compelled to come back to your blog. One of the main ways to stand out is to offer one-of-a-kind content, mixed in frequently. That could mean posting about things you've found elsewhere but adding your own talents or aesthetic for an original twist. For example, Lauren Willhite from Color Collective (see page 23) uses her blog to post inspiring photos she's found online. But she doesn't stop there. She creates a custom color palette for each photo, thus offering an amazing—and totally unique—resource for color inspiration. Similar to how magazines create their content, you should customize as much of your own subject matter as possible. Ideally you should aim for a 50/50 mix of new and existing material, and if you have a higher percentage of your own stuff, even better. Below are some suggestions for bringing original content to your blog.

Use your own images and videos. Just like the editorials you look forward to in your favorite magazines, you, too, can offer your readers custom-created imagery. Capture your soul food recipes with a clear and sharp photo, update your fashion blog by drawing and scanning in your daily outfits, or record simple moments for your lifestyle blog by shooting your own video. Because you're the photographer, videographer, or illustrator and the experience is yours, it's your unique image and content that no one else can duplicate.

Share your life or your work. Sharing parts of your life or work on your blog is something that no one else can replicate, as these experiences or creations are yours alone. By giving readers insight into your creative process or moments from your everyday life, readers are more likely to connect with you on a personal level. Even if the focus of your blog isn't just on your personal life, consider bringing in aspects of your persona or moments from your life when appropriate.

Invent recurring columns. Once you start blogging, you may come up with an idea for an ongoing column or recurring post topic that you can publish weekly or monthly. Maybe it's an interview series with your favorite photographers or a monthly trip to the farmers' market where you document your local finds. Whatever the topic is, in order for it to be a regular feature, it needs to have the potential to be varied enough every week or month while still sticking to the same overall theme or focus. Not only will a regular feature help give you an outline of what to post in upcoming weeks, but readers can also become fans. For example, the "It List" column on SF Girl by Bay features various objects on the wish lists of crafters, stylists, bloggers, and others in the design community. Once you come up with an idea for a regular column, a witty and recognizable title will help reinforce the reoccurring story.

Create your own layouts. While there's nothing wrong with keeping things streamlined and clean by uploading a simple photo tied to your post's content, you can make your blog more unique by posting images that bring together found imagery in an original layout. You can achieve this by familiarizing yourself with programs such as Photoshop or PowerPoint. When I feature roundups or montages on my blog, Oh Joy!, I always lay out the images and objects on a white background with graphic numbers tied to each object. Each time, the theme of the items and the title changes, but the overall look remains consistent. By creating a specific set of graphics and a thematic visual summary, it becomes my own take on a group of existing products.

Secure exclusives. As your readership begins to grow and you interact more with readers, you may begin to develop relationships with various companies, such as owners of small artisanal food stores, or perhaps the PR manager of your favorite home décor shop. They may appreciate how you have spread the word about their company, and may want to keep you in the loop regarding new developments or products, or give you an exclusive look at something new that you can share with your readers. Any time you can offer readers something new that no one else has seen yet, you make your site even more special to them.

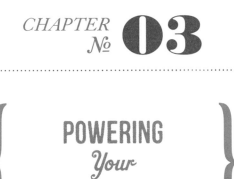

CHAPTER № 03

{ **POWERING** *Your* **BLOG** }

Roll up your sleeves, because this is where the work (and fun) begins: creating your blog! And you'll soon be on your way to blogging up a storm full of amazing ideas. In this chapter we'll dive into how to make your blog come to life—to look, feel, and function however you want it to. You'll see how easy it is to set up a blog through the available blog platforms, learn what kinds of things to post, how to post, and how to come up with a consistent posting schedule to start building reader loyalty. Once you've figured out these steps, you'll wonder why you didn't start a blog sooner!

CHOOSING A *Platform*

Unless you have a background in Web design, it's unlikely that you'll program your blog from scratch. Thankfully, there are a slew of online blogging platforms (also called blog software) that give you the tools to set up a blog. Many of these sites offer easy-to-use templates and a WYSIWYG ("What You See Is What You Get") back-end interface that make delving into the world of blogging much easier and less intimidating. These platforms are available to the public either for free or for a low monthly fee. To further spare your wallet, many blog platforms offer preset themes, or predesigned templates, that you can choose for instant blog design. Following are some of the most popular blog platforms.

Blogger. Blogger tends to be the go-to platform for newbie bloggers because all of its components are free, which makes the investment easier to handle when you don't know exactly where your blog will go. Many people use its predesigned templates as a way to dip their toes into the blogging waters. If you want to customize your site beyond these templates, you'll need a bit of HTML knowledge in order to modify them.

TypePad. If you don't have a lot of time or desire to figure out coding, TypePad provides an easy-to-use platform with a variety of options for creating custom layouts to add images and text. These options are based on how customized you'd like your blog to be, with prices ranging from $9 to $30 per month. If you prefer one-on-one guidance, you can get answers to your questions within twenty-four hours simply by opening up a support ticket through the help center.

Squarespace. Ranging from $12 to $36 a month, Squarespace is also very user-friendly if technical skills aren't your strong suit. A lot of graphic designers and bloggers like its easy-to-use interface because it allows them to design parts of the site themselves, such as headers and buttons, without having to figure out the coding. While most blog platforms have their own statistics trackers, Squarespace's tracker offers more built-in options than others, and is helpful for watching the growth of your blog and seeing where your readers are coming from.

Tumblr. Tumblr makes it easy for its members to immediately find out about your new blog through its existing community and ability to "follow," or "like," other blogs and to "reblog" other blogs' posts within the Tumblr platform. Many larger fashion companies such as Club Monaco, kate spade new york, and J.Crew use Tumblr for their own blogs because of its visual nature, easy setup, and instant community. Signing up for Tumblr is free, and there are a host of free templates within its "Theme Garden" to choose from. Or for something a bit fancier, you can upgrade to a premium template ranging from $9 to $49, or hire a programmer to create a custom theme for you.

WordPress. If you're looking for the flexibility to create any kind of blog you want, from the very basic to the highly customized, WordPress serves both purposes. The software is free, with costs depending on the host you choose and the various plug-ins and themes you download to make your site unique. WordPress allows you to build a completely customized site if you know HTML or CSS and offers a host of plug-ins to help with things like SEO (search engine optimization). It's also a good fit for your budding editorial team, as it allows multiple users to log in as administrators or editors.

Both WordPress and Tumblr offer additional design themes created by freelance programmers and designers, who sell these themes directly to bloggers to use within the two platforms. It's worth it to check out the various themes and templates to figure out what features would be best for your site as well as what costs may be involved—some themes are free, but many come with a price tag of up to $50, depending on the look, functionality, and design.

Also, don't be afraid to ask what blogging platform or themes a fellow blogger uses. If you like the way someone's site looks, he or she might be able to recommend a certain template, blogging platform, or programmer. Whatever platform you choose, make sure that it provides all the features you need, both practically and aesthetically. And remember, if you change your mind in the future, most blogging software offers ways to import your posts from your current blog. The process may not be totally seamless and may require some image resizing and category retagging, but it is possible if you find that you prefer another platform.

Domain NAMES

Once you've chosen a blog platform, it will automatically create a URL for you. For example, the blog A Lovely Day may have the URL www.alovelyday.type pad.com in TypePad or www.alovelyday.blogspot.com in Blogger. However, your site does not need to have the platform's name attached to it. If you don't like the way that looks, you can purchase an alternate URL of your very own. Called "domain mapping," the new domain will simply point to your blog and serve as an alternate address. To do this, first buy the domain name you want from a Web hosting site like Go Daddy or Network Solutions. For a low cost of $10 to $30 per year, the domain name, if available, is yours for the keeping. For example, if www.alovelyday.com is available, you can then point your newly registered domain name to your current blog's URL (the Help section of your blog platform can tell you how to do this). If you

already own a domain for your business and want to have a blog that's connected to your Web site, you can create a subdomain like www.blog .alovelyday.com or www.alovelyday .com/blog, and point this URL to your blog. A *subdomain* is an offshoot of a main site that houses other content (such as your online shop or your portfolio). The benefit of domain mapping is that it's more than just domain forwarding—your URL and all permalinks will contain the address of your new domain, rather than the blog host's domain that you were originally given. In case a domain name is not available, you should think of alternative versions, like www.alovelydayblog.com or www.lovelyday.com. If the domain name you want doesn't seem to be available, that may be a sign that the name is already being used by someone else, in which case you'll want to consider another name so as not to overlap with another blog or business.

DESIGNING *Your* BLOG

The overall look and feel of your blog's design serves as the gateway for the journey you're about to take your readers on. The design should relate to the theme of your site and be a direct reflection of your aesthetic. It shouldn't overwhelm the page or distract from your posts but should complement them instead. One area that should make a statement is the header of your blog. Like the cover of a book, the header gives readers their first impression of your site. The header should include the name of your blog and can also incorporate an interesting image, graphics, or a tagline that elaborates on your subject matter. A craft-focused blog may have a header made up of collaged materials and fabrics, with three-dimensional letters cut out of paper.

{ The design should relate to the theme of your site and be a direct reflection of your aesthetic. }

In contrast, the header for a documentary film blog may be more modern and minimalist, with the logo in a simple font, and a clean layout to place the focus on the black-and-white 8mm films featured. Some newbie bloggers will pull images off photographers' sites and use them to make up their header or business card. This is an absolute no-no. Unless the photographer shot the image for your blog exclusively or has given you permission to use it, copyrighted images should never be used.

If you're unsure about your aesthetic, it's best to stay simple in the beginning. You can always change your custom settings or update to a new blog template as your writing style and aesthetic evolves.

DESIGN HELP

Maybe you'd love to have a crafty, handwritten header or a blog layout that collages multiple images together in a cool way. If you're not an illustrator, graphic designer, or an expert with design programs, you may be at a loss as to how to create that fun header or those unique layouts for your blog. Thankfully, many graphic designers, Web designers, template designers, theme makers, and programmers are out there (with a range of experience and fees) that you can enlist to make your blog look the way you envision it. You can hire someone to design a custom logo, header, blog template, or full-on blog layout for you. If you come across a blog whose design you could stare at for days on end, e-mail the blogger to see who designed their header or site. Then, contact the designer, indicate the items you'd like to have designed, and request an estimate for his or her services. It's best to ask a few of the designers you'd like to work with for an estimate so that you can gauge the range of prices out there. The cost of hiring a designer for just a header or post layout may start at a few hundred dollars, whereas a completely customized blog design will warrant a bigger budget and could start at a few thousand dollars. Decide what's the most feasible for you and your budget. If your blog is still a side hobby, you may choose to save those pennies and just opt for a simple, beautiful header until your readership grows enough to invest in a completely customized site design.

On the flip side, if you've got the time and patience, you can take matters into your own hands and attend a class on Adobe Photoshop or Illustrator to learn how to create interesting headers and layouts yourself. Most local colleges offer basic classes on these programs, so check out next semester's lineup and see what's a good fit for you. You could also enlist a design-savvy friend to give you lessons on how to create designs and layouts specifically for your needs. Finally, you can look for video tutorials online, where you can get all the help you need from the comfort of your own home.

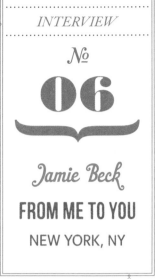

JAMIE BECK often has "pinch me" moments when she thinks about how her career has evolved. A lifelong photographer, Jamie's been capturing the world around her on film ever since she was thirteen years old, when her mom taught her how to use a camera. Following a more traditional photography career path, she attended the Fashion Institute of Technology in New York to study fashion photography, and went on to assist various commercial photographers. While taking a leap of faith into freelancing in 2009, Jamie launched her blog, From Me to You, to archive the images that she had accumulated over the years, and grew a loyal following with her vivid film photos. Then within a couple of years, Jamie and her husband, Kevin, began experimenting with animating her still photos with subtle movements, such as a wisp of hair gently blowing or newspaper pages subtly turning. These "cinemagraphs," as Jamie calls them, debuted on her blog in conjunction with New York Fashion Week in February 2011, taking Jamie's blog and career to a whole new level—her blog readership quickly skyrocketed to more than 60,000 visitors per day. Creating these cinemagraphs, often for luxury fashion clients, is now a full-time job for Jamie and Kevin, all thanks to Jamie's desire to create something new and unexpected for her blog readers.

? *When you started your blog, how did you get people to read it?*

I started by simply being a blog reader. After I had my blog for a little while, I looked at other bloggers I admired and thought about ways to work with them. So I approached Design*Sponge and A Cup of Jo about shooting some photos for them. It was very organic and came out of a true love for their blogs. Once people saw my work on those blogs, other bloggers and readers began to spread the word. It wasn't about money and getting a check; it was about sharing my work and the passion I have for it.

- - - - - ->

How did you come up with the idea to create the cinemagraphs, and why did you decide to make them a main staple of your blog?

I was already shooting and posting still images on my blog. The cinemagraphs came from my desire to create more unique content. In the spring of 2011, Tumblr sent twenty-four bloggers to New York Fashion Week, and I wanted to create something extraordinary for it. I thought about creating videos, but didn't feel like that was different or interesting enough. So Kevin and I started playing around with regular animated gifs. Kevin is a Web designer and used to take clips from TV shows and create funny animated gifs for his blog. Prior to this, we never thought to combine that idea with my still photos. We kept adding more frames to my still photos to make the movements more subtle and kept the entire image still except for one area. This became our first cinemagraph. I posted it right after Fashion Week began, and people responded so well to it. Soon after, I did a collaboration with supermodel Coco Rocha that launched on her Web site and went viral more quickly than I expected. People kept calling it "that thing that you're doing," so we came up with the term "cinemagraphs" so people would know what to call them.

?

What is your process for producing a cinemagraph? How long does it typically take to create one from start to finish?

Wherever we go, we see moments we want to capture—whether it's an everyday image for my blog or something for a client. We always think about each cinemagraph conceptually and want to evoke the right kind of emotions from it. We often plan ahead so that I can shoot the image with an idea of what part will be in motion. For example, I'd shoot a guy in Central Park as well as capture the motion of him flipping through his newspaper, which we'd animate later. Depending on the subject, I could be out for thirty minutes or for a four-hour afternoon of shooting. Sometimes there are surprises, and we'll find other moments in the images later that we didn't anticipate and will focus on instead. Once I come back with the images, Kevin edits them into the final product. It takes him anywhere from four hours to two days to edit and finish one cinemagraph, with one day being about average.

? *Because you've elevated animated gifs in such an elegant way, there must be people who have tried to duplicate this technique. What are your thoughts on that?*

I see it as an art form, and we don't want to be the only people doing it. There's a lot of room for other people to capture the world in this way. What if news photographers were shooting breaking stories like this? It could be so powerful. I want to see other people push the art form differently and in ways that we can't.

? *How has your blog helped your freelance photography career? What opportunities have come to you because of it?*

The blog has changed my career completely and has helped me get noticed by larger companies. We now create pieces for companies like Gilt, Tiffany, Christian Louboutin, Bulgari, the Museum of the City of New York, and Oscar de la Renta. We're also working on more online editorial content for magazines like *Details* and *Lucky*. It's been great, but so overwhelming, too.

? *You also design Tumblr templates that people can purchase and use. Why did you decide to offer that service?*

I received so many requests from people who wanted my blog's design. I didn't want to give them the same design I was using, so Kevin and I figured out a way to offer them custom themes. It's really expensive to hire a Web designer to design and program a site from scratch, so we wanted to give bloggers a lower-priced option with our templates. The templates are designs that the average girl who reads my site would like—they're a bit romantic and nostalgic. I understand what that type of reader and blogger likes, so I'll art direct what details should go on the template design, and Kevin designs and programs it.

? *How has blogging changed your life?*

I have way less time to kill now; but in a good way, of course. Everything in my life has turned into a potential photo shoot—dinners, vacations, etc. It's

- - - - - →

funny that I now have to ask my family and friends to sign model releases, because I may end up printing or publishing their image at some point. If the moment is beautiful, it has to be captured.

? *What do you love most about blogging?*

I think of blogging like modern dance—it's very free-form and has no one direction or method. I love how you can change and grow your blog with the demand and feedback you receive from readers. In photography or fashion, there was always a set of rules you had to follow to get to where you wanted to go. But now with blogging, you can define who you are, what you do, and what your vision is. Because I came from a traditional background as a photographer, I had to erase my way of thinking to be open to these opportunities that came through the work I created on my blog. Had I not started my blog, all of these amazing things wouldn't have happened.

WRITING A *Compelling* BIO

When readers come across a blog that catches their eye, they're inclined to be curious about the person behind the blog and want to know more about you. The "About" section of your blog should tell readers a bit about you and the inspiration behind your blog and its content. A short and sweet bio is always best. You can write it in first person or third person, depending on what fits your voice best. Usually, personal blogs will have bios written in first person, whereas blogs that are more topic-based or an extension of a business will have bios written in third person. If you'd rather not share your story on a full page, you can place a shorter statement on your sidebar accompanied by a photo. For example, "Jane Smith is a photographer, writer, and mother living in Denver who shares her inspirations daily on her Point and Shoot blog." If you've chosen to remain anonymous on your blog, readers would still like to learn about when and why your blog started, even if you decide not to share your name or likeness with them.

It should be noted that a photo isn't always necessary, but it does help readers connect with you when they can see the face behind their favorite daily read. When including a photo of yourself, make sure it's professional, clear, and evokes the mood of your blog—whether serious, earthy, or quirky. That doesn't mean you have to spend hundreds of dollars for head shots from a professional photographer. If your budget doesn't allow for a photo-snapping pro, ask a friend with a steady hand and a decent digital camera to take photos of you in front of a colorful wallpapered wall, in your kitchen

{ When including a photo of yourself, make sure it's professional, clear, and evokes the mood of your blog . . . }

whipping up some treats, in your carpentry workshop, or in another setting that hints at your blog's content. Cropped casual photos from the beach or the bar are not advised. Also, remember that your grandpa may read your blog, so be tasteful (no cleavage!) and put your best face forward. If you've chosen to remain slightly anonymous, you can include a whimsical photo that doesn't give you away. For example, the About page on your foodie blog may show your face hidden behind a large cheeseburger with only your eyes exposed, or as a book blogger, you may be shot from the back while perusing stacks of your favorite books.

WHAT TO *Post*

There are probably a plethora of ideas swirling around your head that would make perfect fodder for a blog post. Whether a roundup of summer beauty products, a kids' birthday-party table setup, a DIY video on how to make a wooden candelabra, or a thoughtful essay on love and marriage—the options for content are endless. Now, if your creative juices aren't flowing yet and you're not sure exactly what you want to post, try keeping a note-book with you at all times for jotting down ideas, or recording your thoughts into the memo section of your smartphone when they pop into your head. By having a place to store these lightbulb moments, you'll be less likely to have to force yourself to come up with ideas on the spot. Also, surround yourself with inspiration outside of your computer. Visit museums, take a cooking class, read a new book or magazine, and take weekend trips to fun destinations. All of these things will naturally provide an inspiration that will turn into bigger ideas for your blog. To help you out, here are some types of things you might post about.

№1 *Diary*

This is a personal chronicle of your life or your thoughts about life. If friends and family members will be included (either in photos or by name), make sure they are okay with being featured on your blog, and ask if there are any circumstances under which they'd feel uncomfortable being a part of it. Because these types of posts focus on the writing, begin penning your thoughts as they come naturally, and make sure to edit, proofread, and spell-check to ensure you're putting your best writing foot forward.

№2 *Mood Boards*

If you're working on a thematic roundup to cite your inspirations for the best new makeup trends, your budding backyard wonderland, or items for your trip to Greece, browsing the Internet for possible items to include will become your favorite new hobby. Whether showing products or tear sheets of photographed images, always credit the site and source where you found the image so that readers can know where to buy it or who created or photographed it (see page 95).

№3 *Tutorials*

If your blog concept requires you to produce a recipe, a DIY craft, or a detailed description of your favorite place setting, be prepared to give both visual and written directions on how to concoct your signature blood-orange lollipops, make a Christmas stocking, or pull together a summer-themed table setting. Once these images have been captured, you'll have a base of supporting pictures to begin building your blog post and giving readers a step-by-step tour into your process. If you plan to feature a lot of tutorials, it's best to offer how-to's with varying levels of difficulty so that those who are less crafty feel as though there are simpler options they can follow as well.

№ 4 Portfolio Updates

In addition to seeing your newest work, readers often like to see pieces that didn't make the cut and aren't shown on your professional Web site. Maybe you created a stop-motion animation for a client and have extra footage that didn't make the final version. By posting these out-takes, you can share other things you've created that might not be available anywhere else but still show your innate style and talent.

№ 5 Shop or Business Updates

Similar to portfolio updates, if your blog is being used to help market your business, provide behind-the-scenes details from the building of your new store, special discounts for blog readers, or online shop updates when they occur.

№ 6 Reviews

Some blogs focus on sharing the best of their favorite discoveries with others. Whether it's a hot new gastropub, the greatest gadget for multitasking at work, or a must-have bronzer, talk about products in your own voice and in a way that readers can relate to and enjoy. Depending on the type of products you're reviewing, you may even consider doing a video review to show the functionality or use of something that can't be described as well with words and static images alone.

№ 7 Submissions

Some blogs' concepts are heavily based on reader submissions. Maybe you post about all the silly typos found in billboards or newspaper ads, or have a blog about hot dogs from around the world. When your content is made stronger with the help of readers from around the world, be sure to state how people can send you their submissions so that you constantly have new material to keep up with your clever curation.

Since some posts (especially tutorials or diary-like entries) can be lengthy, with lots of images and text, you can truncate these so readers see only the first couple of images or the first paragraph of text, and can then click on "Read More" to see the full post. By adding a page break to your post, you'll avoid having one post take up the majority of your front-page space and also make it easier for readers to see the posts that come before and after it. The back end of your blog platform will usually have an icon that you can click while composing a post to insert this "break" wherever you see fit.

Remember that you also don't want to bombard your readers with too many posts a day. The ability to edit is a blessing. If you have ten post ideas brewing in your mind, write them all down and take a hard look at which are really blog-worthy—maybe there's content there for six really solid posts that you can schedule over two weeks. Whatever content you end up creating, it's always best to give readers a mix of both long and short posts to vary both the visuals and the amount of text and images they'll see.

BOOKMARK IT!

When trolling the World Wide Web for blogging inspiration, you'll find yourself bookmarking items for potential future posts like crazy. Some people choose to use their browser's bookmark tool and save links into separate folders based on theme. But now there are easy and helpful online image-saving tools, such as Pinterest, FFFFOUND!, Svpply, Evernote, and Gimme Bar that make it even easier to save, organize, and view your inspirations along the way. You will slowly build a collection of images that may become a part of, or inspire, a future post. If you're using a public site (like Pinterest) where others can view and add your saved images to their own boards, make sure to save all your images under that site's permalink (so the original source can always be found), and add explanatory text crediting where the image came from and who created it, photographed it, or blogged it originally. That way, as it makes its way around the Internet, the original source will be attached.

ADDING *Images* TO YOUR POST

Whether your posts involve full journal entries or simple one-liners, images can have more impact than words alone and give readers a visual to get excited about. The images within your posts could be your original photographs of last night's dinner, scans of the latest fabric swatches you'll be turning into a quilt, or a mood board that incorporates items for decorating your baby's nursery. When you set up your blog's template, you are usually given a choice of the width size of your main column. This is the column where your main content will live, so decide if you'd prefer that area to be larger (which works great for very visual blogs) or more narrow (which works well for text-heavy blogs). Main column widths typically range from 400 pixels to 600 pixels wide. The width is up to you; choose a size that you think will give your words or images the most impact.

To keep the aesthetic of your site consistent, make the width of your images the same width as your posts. For example, if you've set your main text column to a width of 600 pixels, you should make all of your images 600 pixels wide as well. Also, stay consistent with how your text and images fit together. Whether your commentary comes before or after an image, it should be in the same order for each post so that readers get used to the way

{ To keep the aesthetic of your site consistent, make the width of your images the same width as your posts. }

you present your posts. And be sure to always keep the same text justification: Don't use left-justified text in one post and centered text in another. That way when a reader looks at your blog, their eye is drawn downward seamlessly without any jarring changes in text justification or image size.

Sometimes you'll come across an image online that you want to post that is smaller than the size you'd like it to be. Unfortunately, you can't stretch a 400-pixel-wide image to 600 pixels, or it will appear pixilated, or blurry. Instead, make sure you're shooting photos or scanning images that are

larger than you'll need (it's always better to scale down than up) or pull images that are at least 600 pixels wide. Search for the largest version of an image, either through a Google search or using the magnified version of an image that some Web sites offer. If the image simply doesn't exist in a larger version, then perhaps you can create an inspiration board or a montage that makes good use of the smaller image and combines it with a few others in the same theme. You can play around with layering color and type, or tilting the images using design programs like Photoshop, Illustrator, or InDesign. If you don't have those programs available, you can also use PowerPoint to create a unique layout. Once you've created the layout, save the original layered version in case you want to go back later and make changes. Save all final images as either a jpeg or gif to be uploaded into your post—jpegs are typically the format used for low-resolution flat image files, while gifs are usually for animated images.

COME ON, GET *Snappy*

As a budding blogger, you'll soon realize that many moments of your life (whether last night's dinner, today's outfit, or the blooming jacaranda trees) will become blog-worthy topics. So get used to carrying your camera wherever you go, and be ready to pull it out when inspiration hits!

Whether you use a digital SLR, a point-and-shoot, or a high-megapixel camera phone, crisp and clear photos are key to putting the best original images on your blog. You'll know you've captured a great moment when your photo makes a reader want to dive headfirst into that ice cream sundae you just ate. No one wants to see a blurry or dark image, even if you took the photo yourself. When serving as your own photographer, a few basics will help you get your point (and shoot) across.

№ 1 *Shoot a Few Versions*

Nothing's worse than capturing the perfect moment, only to discover later that the image was blurry or that a car drove through the frame when you didn't realize it. So it's always a good idea to take at least a few images of the same subject. Try zooming in and out, and play with a couple of different angles, too—that way when you go home and review your photo session, you can choose the best of the bunch.

№ 2 *Stick to Daylight*

Daylight photos shot in indirect light are always best and are the most flattering for photographs of people, nature, and food. When you're not a professional and don't know how to change your camera's manual settings or put up fancy lighting, it's better not to add variables like extreme glare or dark shadows to the mix. Daylight photos will give you the optimal canvas to work off of.

№ 3 *Experiment with Composition*

Subjects tend to look best when they are not smack dab in the middle of the frame. In art speak, the "rule of thirds" is when a subject is closer to one side of the frame. Imagine dividing the image into thirds, either horizontally or vertically. The subject should sit in between the first two thirds or last two thirds of the image. So experiment both with centering and with having your subject sit slightly off to the side of your viewfinder.

№ 4 *Learn to Edit*

After downloading your newest batch of photos to your computer, you'll want to choose the best images. After that you may need to take it one step further and narrow them down even more. If you're showcasing your latest floral arrangement, readers can get a better sense of the story with a full-on photo of the blooms plus a couple of different detail shots. They won't need to see the same arrangement in front of four different backgrounds. As much as you'll want to show off every image that you love, remember to show only what's needed to tell the story simply and beautifully. You can always upload the outtakes to a Flickr page or an album on your Facebook fan page and direct readers there to see more.

№ 5 Crop and Retouch

Despite your best efforts at shooting in natural daylight or having your subject sit slightly off center, sometimes a photo can come out different than you intended. Have no fear! As long as the image is clear and tells a good story about the subject, you can make some minor adjustments to your photos using Photoshop or iPhoto. Simply crop out any unnecessary background (like your cat's tail, which snuck its way into the scene) or use the brightness and contrast filters to brighten up an overcast image.

№ 6 Keep the Originals

You'll be sizing your final picks to 72 dpi (best for Web resolution), but you never know when you'll need the original high-resolution version of the images you posted. Perhaps you'll want to make an image into a postcard or will need the photos for a future book project!

№ 7 Take a Photography Class

If you want to learn about lighting, apertures, or the various settings on your camera, a basic photography class can be really helpful. Whether a class at a local college or a one-on-one tutorial with a photographer you admire, learning more about how to take a better photo will always be to your blog's benefit.

MOTION PICTURES

Blog possibilities get more exciting by the minute. In addition to photos and images, you can also publish sound bites, videos, and short films on your blog. Is your message better communicated through spoken narrative? If so, record and post a podcast (an audio or video recording), such as your interview with friends about their favorite summer memories. Are you a Giada De Laurentiis in the making? Then have a friend record the pilot of your very own cooking show to share with your readers. Andrea Pippins of Fly gives her readers a front seat to her adventures out and about as she shops at local flea markets and vintage stores. Her "webisodes" illustrate what she finds and how she ends up making those finds into an outfit all her own. If you enjoy the moving picture more than the still version, maybe your blog will turn into a "vlog" (a "video blog") and exist purely as video content. You can record videos on a handheld digital camcorder, with a digital SLR that has video, from your computer's camera, or even with your smartphone. Then simply upload your masterpiece to YouTube or Vimeo, embed the videos into your blog using the code provided, and you're on your way to providing readers with a multisensory experience!

№

07

Amy Cao

AMY BLOGS CHOW

NEW YORK, NY

LIKE MANY ON-THE-GO NEW YORKERS, **Amy Cao** barely used her kitchen. While her food writing and editing jobs at Zagat, offManhattan, and Tasting Table had given her plenty of highbrow eating experiences to write about, her role as cook in her Manhattan apartment was not so accomplished. Looking to be a more active participant in her kitchen, Amy tried to re-create a banana milkshake from one of her favorite local restaurants. After a few tries, she finally had a successful outcome. She filmed a short video showing how to make the frosty treat and posted it on her blog, Amy Blogs Chow. Up until then, her blog was largely a portfolio of her food writing, but because of the popularity of the video, she made how-to's showing people how to make other simple snacks, and her online video series, "Stupidly Simple Snacks," was born. The videos are now the main draw of her blog, as the series teaches the cooking deficient how to create snack staples like baked potatoes and deviled eggs and even trendy desserts like ice cream lollipops. Amy's natural charm is apparent in her three-minute clips, complete with endearing, unedited hiccups and bloopers. Armed with a simple and original idea, Amy shows that you don't need a ton of technical tricks up your sleeve to create original and happiness-inducing content.

? *What's the concept and thought process behind your videos?*

Most cooking shows and videos are all about perfection and showing really fancy things, but no one was poking fun at being a New Yorker who never uses their kitchen. When I show people how to make things, I explain it in a way that people with no cooking background can understand. I show every detail of how something is done, even if it seems obvious and simple, like flour being dumped into a bowl. If I come across a recipe that deters me from cooking, I think of a way to show it in the clearest way possible. It's not a manicured process, so the videos are blooper-filled. Things definitely get messy, but I think that's what people like about it. Living in New York, you don't always have the space and right equipment, so I think of how to make every recipe and episode easy and approachable.

How did you figure out how to talk on camera as well as the process for shooting and editing your videos?

It started with me and the video camera that came with my computer, and today it is still very much like that. I didn't take any classes; I just learned as I went and taught myself iMovie on my MacBook. Now that the series has grown, it's evolved a bit. I've hired a video editor, and I'll probably get a high-definition camera soon. But I still want the videos to have a homemade feel. I like the idea that I can shoot it myself and I'm not depending on a crew of people to be there every time I want to shoot a new one.

What opportunities have come from your blog?

My blog gave me the opportunity to write for various online food sites and to eventually join the team at Foodspotting. I like the idea of collaborating on something I believe in, so I joined the startup Foodspotting, and I've been working for them full-time since January 2011 as Head of Community. I handle the content for their Web site and all their social media and make all their videos. And when I started my blog, my greatest dream was to make videos with people in the food community whom I admire and take it on the road, and now I've had the chance to do that!

How do you find the time to maintain your blog with a full-time job?

When I started working full-time, I quickly realized that it would be a challenge to maintain what was essentially two sites—my WordPress blog and my Tumblr site. I liked how easy it was to blog on the go with Tumblr, so I decided to go exclusively with that platform, which let me stay in touch with readers whether I was sitting at my desk at home, at a crawfish boil in Brooklyn, or walking around Rome looking for gelato.

- - - - - ->

I began posting pieces that were more vignettes than lengthy articles, with the goal of including my readers in my day as a food lover in New York, and also to make it a bit more feasible for me to post with less time. For me, embracing my role at Foodspotting meant less time for my blog, but Amy Blogs Chow is now a more focused diary, scrapbook, and home for "Stupidly Simple" snack videos. With my full-time job, I now update my blog three to four times a week and focus more on quality over quantity.

? *You now often feature New York chefs in your videos. How do you go about approaching them?*

Now that I have a pretty strong following, many chefs or those in the food industry approach me 90 percent of the time! It's usually through word of mouth or something like "My friend has this business and would love to do a video with you," or a chef's PR person will approach me. Also, I'm doing them not just with chefs, but also with other food lovers, bloggers, and people that simply inspire me.

? *Do your videos earn income for you?*

When my blog began, I was already earning consistent income through freelance writing. But once I decided to do videos, I knew they wouldn't earn money immediately. So I moved in with my boyfriend to save on rent so I could really focus on the quality of content and not how I could make money right away.

? *What's the most fun aspect of having a food blog?*

Oh, there are so many. I'd say the best parts are connecting with other people I think are awesome, having a forum to share the things that I like, and knowing that I made someone laugh or feel better that day. The more social media becomes mainstream, the more chances we have to create something from nothing and tell a story. I love relating to people and making food approachable for them. Having my blog and creating my videos for it is just another way of connecting with people and turning these online conversations into stronger connections.

FREQUENCY *of* POSTS

Once readers find your blog and love what they see, they are apt to come back regularly to see what's new in your corner of the Internet. Most seasoned bloggers post at least once a day during the week (from Monday to Friday), and some widely read blogs with multiple contributors, like The Dieline, post four to six times a day. Daily posts ensure that when a reader returns on any given day, they are seeing something new. However, five posts a week can certainly seem like a lot for a fresh-faced blogger. If you can't commit to daily posts, consistency is key in keeping your readers interested and coming back for more. If you're juggling a part-time job and your toddler's nap schedule, maybe two to three times a week is more feasible for you. If that's the case, you should allot certain days of the week for the posts to appear—like Monday, Wednesday, and Friday. That way readers will be accustomed to your post routine. (You can even mention your posting schedule on your About page so that readers know when to tune in.) When it comes to what time of the day to post, it's up to you. Some bloggers like to post at times when readers are most likely to be browsing the Internet, like first thing in the morning or during lunch breaks. But since your readers will likely be in different time zones from one another, simply pick the times that are best for you and stick to these times consistently every time you post. The quickest way to lose a regular reader is for them to come to your site a week or two later or more, and not see a new post. They'll soon assume you're no longer blogging and will find other blogs to follow who do update regularly.

PLANNING *Ahead* AND BLOGGING FROM *Afar*

Let's say your full-time work schedule only makes it possible for you to blog on weekends, but you want to have the posts go live during the week. Almost all blogging platforms allow you to schedule your blog posts in advance so they can appear on specific days and times without the need for you to be at your desk the very moment your newest entry goes live. This is a great way to work in advance as well if you'll be going on vacation or are away from a computer for an extended period of time. Posting in advance allows you to be away without your readers noticing any posting delays or interruptions. Also, a recurring column can help you gather regular content for future posts, making it easier to plan ahead and also to build reader loyalty through consistent topics.

Many blog platforms have mobile versions that allow you to create new blog posts remotely from your smartphone or handheld device (like an iPad), and some programs even give you the option to post by sending your content to an e-mail address. Most remote blogging platforms are best for simple posts. Anything requiring a special layout or lots of text with many links might be more difficult to control. However, having the option to blog remotely comes in handy when you find yourself with a quick burst of inspiration outside the office or you want to send your readers a short message (like something came up and you'll be back soon).

ESTABLISHING A *Creative* WORKSPACE

When you're starting out, you may not be making much or any money from your blog. Luckily, many bloggers can work from the comfort of their own home—you could even work in your pajamas on a small area of your couch. The low overhead and convenience of a home-based workspace makes it a financially sensible location.

No matter where you set up your blogging headquarters, it helps to set the stage for creativity. Prepare a large bulletin board or inspiration wall where you can attach swatches, images, and photos for blog ideas you're working on. Even though most of your work will exist virtually, it's nice to step away and look at some real-life inspiration when your eyes need a break from that illuminated screen. While initially you may only need a computer, be sure to give yourself enough space to comfortably add a scanner, printer, camera, or any other blogging tools to help you create your posts. If you don't have a room, like an extra bedroom or basement, for a separate office, then define your space using bookshelves or room dividers—particularly if you share an apartment or house with roommates or your family. By keeping your blogging space as separate as possible, you'll be more focused when it's time to blog and less distracted by any other people who may be around you. Once you've turned your home into a blogging-friendly place, your productivity is likely to be at its best.

APP TO IT!

You're a blogger—so you gotta love modern technology. For one, it's allowed our phones to be cameras, giving us the ability to capture unique photos without fancy equipment or years of training. There are a slew of applications (commonly called "apps") that allow you to take a simple snapshot with your camera phone and then process it through a filter to make it look retro, monochromatic, high-contrast, or even like a real Polaroid. Some of my favorite apps include Instagram, CrossProcess, myFilm, Hipstamatic, ShakeItPhoto, Picfx, Grid Lens, and Frametastic. You can also become an instant filmmaker with apps like 8mm, which turn your recorded video into an old-timey silent film or a monochromatic documentary. Best of all, many of these programs allow you to save the final image or video to your phone's archive, e-mail it to yourself, or connect directly to Facebook, Twitter, or Flickr so you can share the image with others. Since new apps come out every day, you can stay abreast by checking your phone's app store or marketplace regularly for what's new, or subscribing to tech blogs like TechCrunch that feature new apps when they launch.

CHAPTER
№ 04

{ **BLOGGING**
Community
ETIQUETTE }

Once you've published your blog, it's out on the Internet for all to see, read, and adore. You now have a virtual place to connect with like-minded people for an open dialogue about your common interests, aesthetics, or style of work. Interacting with others who share a passion with you, such as making custom bicycles, can be invaluable to your growth not only as a budding bike maker, but also as a new member of the blogging world. In order to start expanding your community, potential readers need to know you exist. You must therefore take an active part in promoting your blog and increasing your community of readers, who will then help spread the word about it and support you in your new endeavor. Building and maintaining your community is just as important as coming up with a great new post and should be given the same care and attention. In this chapter, you will learn how to grow your base of readers, approach other bloggers without spamming their inboxes, use comments to build your community, navigate through the social media tools, and properly credit those you post about.

BE *Active* ONLINE

While you may have started your blog to share your point of view on modern-day woodworking with the world, you should also read other blogs, especially those you think would enjoy your blog as well. Leave constructive and fun comments on these blogs and follow them on Twitter or Facebook. Soon their readers (as well as the blogs' editors) may begin to take notice and click over to your site.

However, keep in mind that leaving a comment on a blog post or a Facebook fan page isn't just about dropping links to your blog. While this

may be an opportunity to promote your blog, it might be considered "spamming" if you leave a comment or message just to advertise your site. Doing this can be seen as leaving unsolicited promotional material (just like the pizza delivery flyer hanging on your front door knob). Instead, put your blog's URL in the box allotted for Web site links, not the comment box. You can even sign your name (e.g., "Jane from A Lovely Day"), and if others want to know more about you, they can click on your name to be redirected to your blog.

CONTACT YOUR *Fellow* BLOGGERS

New bloggers are often wary of contacting other bloggers, especially more established ones, to tell them about their site. While you may be intimidated, remember that all bloggers (no matter how big they may seem now) started with zero readers and zero comments. So they should certainly understand where you're coming from. Send a simple and genuine e-mail letting these bloggers know how much you enjoy their blogs, how they've inspired you, and include a link to your blog in hopes that they'll check it out.

Also, blogs often have a "blogroll" in their side column that lists the blogs they read on a regular basis. To get on some blogrolls, it might be easier to start by connecting with newer bloggers whom you respect and seeing if

{ A blog's readership grows through the cumulative traffic that comes to its site, so if you share links with blogs you like, chances are they will do the same for you. }

they'd like to exchange links with you. A blog's readership grows through the cumulative traffic that comes to its site, so if you share links with blogs you like, chances are they will do the same for you. If you try to contact a bigger blog, however, it's likely that they get tons of e-mails daily and may not have time to respond. But you never know—they may include a link to your blog in a future post or tell their Twitter or Facebook followers about you. If they do, be sure to send them a quick thank-you for their kind support.

CONTACT THOSE YOU'VE FEATURED

If you've profiled an up-and-coming modern artist or an artisanal choco-latier, send them a link to your post with a short and sweet e-mail letting them know that you admire their work and have featured them on your blog. These artists or artisans may not always be aware of every blog or press mention they receive, so they'll love hearing from you and appre-ciate that you shared their story with your readers. They may even post your story on their own blog, Facebook, or Twitter pages, which could bring potential new fans your way.

CONTRIBUTE *to* OTHER BLOGS

If you're an expert at cake decorating and notice that a larger food blog often posts about dessert but hasn't shown a technique that you're skilled at, be proactive and contact the blog editor about potentially guest blogging for their site or perhaps collaborating on a project that you both can blog about. Typically guest blogging is a one-time or infrequent occurrence. Blog editors may ask other bloggers to write posts for when they go on vacation or maternity leave as a way to continue to provide readers with interesting content while they're away. Sometimes guest blogs fill a void and become a popular feature on a site, with the blogger turning into a regularly paid contributor, bringing his or her area of expertise to the blog on a weekly or monthly basis.

Collaborating on a joint project with another blogger (especially one with a complementary talent) is another option. For example, if you're a photographer and you know a blogger who's a prop stylist, you could work together to create a series of color-themed vignettes for each month of the year. You might gather objects together—red objects one month, yellow another, and so on—and she might style them while you photograph them. The ongoing project could make fun fodder for both of your blogs and bring your two talents together to create something new and beautiful. Both types of relationships can be beneficial in increasing your name recognition in the community and helping to bring additional traffic to your site.

Geninne D. Zlatkis

GENINNE'S ART BLOG

QUERÉTARO, MEXICO

THANKS TO HER MOTHER, who owned an art gallery in Chile, Geninne Zlatkis's passion for art was instilled in her as a toddler, and from then on, she could be found drawing and painting up a storm. Despite studying both architecture and graphic design in college, Geninne was most drawn to painting and crafting. She began sending her drawings to the blog Illustration Friday, where readers submit work based on a weekly theme. Because submissions required having your own blog, she started hers, called Geninne's Art Blog, in 2005 and continued to create a drawing a week for two years based on those assignments. Geninne credits her blog and Illustration Friday for helping her to develop her style and talent as an artist. She believes that the constant practice and motivation to share with others has helped her talent evolve and grow to a place she never imagined it could.

? *What do you share on your blog?*

I create almost every single day for myself. I'm very crafty, and making things is something that I have to do to keep my sanity! So I always have material to share on the blog—sometimes it's a project I am working on for a client, and other times it's something I am doing for fun. Having the blog motivates me to constantly share the work I'm making and get feedback from readers. I think it's important to stay consistent, so I try to post every day. If I do go away for a break, I'll let readers know ahead of time.

When I first started showing my work, many readers would ask how I made something or what supplies I used. So now I always talk about the materials, like if there are iron-ons that I'm embroidering, I'll tell people where to get them in addition to telling my process. I really try to put as much information on there ahead of time to answer readers' potential questions. I started offering videos of some of my DIY projects, because they

-----→

were better demonstrated than described. My hand-carved stamp tutorial is really popular, and I have a series of watercolor videos that show me painting. I also create a monthly desktop calendar that people can download for free. I love giving back to my readers because they enrich my experience with their feedback and support.

What types of career opportunities have come to you because of your blog?

I'm thankful that all of my clients have arrived through the blog. I've never had an agent, so companies find me through it and e-mail me about working together. I work with a few companies like Galison, Urban Outfitters, and Hallmark in the United States, which license my art. I also do a lot of book cover illustrations. I have a fabric line with Cloud9 Fabrics and wrote a book on stamping with Lark Books. In addition to my client work and my blog, I have an Etsy shop where I sell prints of my watercolors and a Big Cartel shop where I sell originals of my art.

Why did you decide to start your online shop? What made you choose Etsy and Big Cartel to sell your work?

When I started doing Illustration Friday, I wanted to sell some of the illustrations that seemed to be popular, so I started a CafePress shop. It was not successful at all, so I closed it and forgot about it for a while. I started doing more illustrations on my blog and was doing a "Bird a Day" series. They were watercolor birds painted on top of vintage ephemera. When that series was finished, it was super-popular, so I decided to open an Etsy shop to sell prints of the twenty illustrations in the series. I wanted to be able to sell my work directly and not through another site that would print it for me, so I bought a professional archival-quality printer and hoped to make back what I spent on it. When I put the prints up for sale, I sold through in one day three times what I spent on the printer! Now, I still have my Etsy shop because of the amazing community there and the people that can find your shop through their treasuries and posts. But when I sell originals, I prefer to use Big Cartel, because their fees are lower than Etsy's, and that's helpful for my higher-priced items. Whenever I have new original pieces to add to my shop, I tell readers ahead of time, and they usually sell quickly because people really like having a one-of-a-kind piece.

How has blogging influenced your work as an artist?

Blogging has made me more consistent in my work. I've gotten a lot of encouraging comments from my readers that keep me motivated to keep creating stuff. It's like fuel for me. I also love reading comments from people who have been following me since the beginning, because they see how I've evolved as an artist. It's inspiring for them as well to see what can happen over time. The secret to developing your style is time and a lot of practice. You have to constantly hone your craft.

How has having your blog and career at home made it easier to be more active in your children's lives?

I knew I wanted to homeschool my children before I even had any. It's been a dream come true for me to be able to stay committed to their learning while nurturing my own creative life. I'm a complete homebody, so it's great to have those two worlds together under our cozy roof.

Has anything unexpected come from having your blog?

After seeing my art and watching me work on my site, my fourteen-year-old son, Daniel, decided to start a blog and is also selling his artwork in my Etsy shop! I initially linked to his pet portraits on my blog, but he got so many inquiries and so much interest that he decided to start his own blog. He came to me one day and asked if he could make a blog, and I told him that would be a fun idea. He created the banner by scanning in his own artwork and set up the site, Daniel Does, all by himself. Sometimes he gets overwhelmed keeping up with the sales and will take a break, but he loves it. It's also been great for him to develop his writing and spelling skills. Now he has his own followers and his own set of customers.

INITIATE A LOCAL BLOGGER *Meet-Up*

A blogger's life is spent in front of a computer, often in the solitude of her home. Since face-to-face connections may be few and far between, initiating a local blogger meet-up in your area can be a great way for you to meet others going through the same trials and tribulations of being a budding blogger. You can reach out to other bloggers in your area over e-mail, post an

> Since face-to-face connections may be few and far between, initiating a local blogger meet-up in your area can be a great way for you to meet others going through the same trials and tribulations of being a budding blogger.

announcement on your blog, or see who else would be interested via Twitter. You'll see how many others crave the same interaction that you do, and you may soon have a small group that you can regularly call on to seek advice, support one another, or simply hang out with as friends. As with any type of group activity, someone should be in charge of getting the group together regularly. So whether you want to take the reins or have an organizer that changes monthly, the blogger in charge of each meet-up can come up with topics to discuss, a fun restaurant to meet at, or some sort of exercise or blog post for everyone to finish by the monthly meeting time.

PREPARE YOUR *Cocktail Party* SPIEL

Talking about your blog in person can be hard to do without the aid of visuals or a laptop. But remember that making real-life connections is important, too. Whether you're at a blog conference or your spouse's holiday party, always be prepared with a succinct description of your blog that tells others why you started it, what you blog about, and why it's fun and different. You can say something like "My blog, Punchy Party, is all about bringing color to any celebratory occasion. I've always loved coming up with ideas for parties and used to find myself scribbling ideas on napkins and at my desk during work all the time. So I started my blog to flesh out those ideas and share them with others! Whether it's a birthday party, wedding, or simply to celebrate a new job, I like to share ideas about things you can bake or create to make it a special and colorful event. For example, I show how to make things like a rainbow-layered cake or how to set a table all in one color theme."

CREATE BUSINESS CARDS

While you may not (yet) see your blog as a business, you should still spread the word about it by having business cards made with your logo or header, Web site URL, and e-mail address. You can call on the assistance of a design-savvy friend to help you with this task, employ the designer who created your header, or create your business cards yourself using any design programs you've learned. Once you have a layout together, you can have them printed in a few different ways. For example, you can enlist a letterpress, offset, or digital printer to make multiples of your new calling card. Letterpress is often the most costly method and requires larger printing minimums (around 500 pieces to make the cost worth it). So if you'd prefer to spend a bit less or want to start with a smaller number of cards, digital or offset printing would be a more feasible option for you. There are online printing sites like 4by6 .com where you can upload your artwork, choose various quantities and finishes, approve a PDF (Portable Document Format) of the card, and have the printed cards in your hands sometimes in less than a week. Now with your fancy new cards in hand, any time you mention your blog or find that someone wants to know more, you can give them a card to direct them to where to find you online.

THE SOCIAL *Network*

Social networking may seem completely overwhelming when you're first immersing yourself in this world of virtual sharing and communication. But the good thing is that with a blog, you've already acquainted yourself with social networking. To continually grow your blog, readership, community, and presence online, participating in other social media outlets is essential. There's an array of social media platforms out there—from the more known, like Facebook and Twitter, to those that are more niche, like Pinterest and Instagram—that can be very powerful tools for creative types.

FACEBOOK

Almost everyone these days (including your dad and your twelve-year-old niece) has a personal Facebook page. You can reach those who frequent Facebook by starting a fan page for your blog. Your personal life and your blog life could be one and the same, or you could separate them so that you have a personal page for people you know and have actually met and a fan page for anyone you don't know personally who wants to connect with you. I typically recommend limiting your personal page to those you actually know in real life. You never know what tagged photos of you may show up on your page (blog fans do not need to see bikini-clad photos of you on vacation in Maui) or personal messages from your high school friends that may pop up on your wall. With a Facebook fan page, you can even have your posts

{ I typically recommend limiting your personal page to those you actually know in real life. }

automatically linked to it (using an application like NetworkedBlogs), offering your fans another avenue for engagement with you. When updating your Facebook fan page, give readers other informational gems they wouldn't otherwise see on your blog. The fan page is a tool that not only allows for text information, but also lets you post photos and videos. Ask readers what their favorite color is if you're seeking inspiration for your next color-themed post, or upload outtakes from your fashion blog's style shots that didn't make the cut. Also, be sure to check your Facebook fan page often to see what readers are saying about you or asking you. As the gatekeeper to your community, you want to play an active role in these conversations.

TWITTER

Similar to posting a status update on your wall in Facebook, Twitter is a way to communicate with your followers by sharing your thoughts, links to photos or Web sites, or anything else you want to relay. Except in this case, your messages are limited to 140 characters—so it's all about sharing bits of information that can be conveyed within that limited space. Small businesses, movie stars, and even the president "tweet" (communicate via Twitter) with their customers or fans. If you're following an interior designer who is on a reality show, that designer might send live tweets during the episodes, sharing his thoughts on what he was really thinking during each challenge to give his fans insight into his process. Or an architect could upload photos to Twitter giving potential clients glimpses of a home she's designing to demonstrate what she could create for their dream house. And, unlike the process of friending people on Facebook, you can freely follow whomever you want, as long as their Twitter account is open to the public. If you're not by a computer all day, you can use an application like HootSuite to schedule your tweets in advance. But remember not to make them sound too mechanical, as spur-of-moment tweets often feel the most authentic. Twitter is best used in combination with your blog when you include the following:

> **Updates from your blog.** At a minimum, you should always link new posts to your Twitter feed so that followers are reminded to check out your newest entry. Many readers use Twitter as a way to keep track of blogs they like and will click over to your new posts once they're alerted that there's something new to see.

- **Links to sites featuring things you like or find helpful.** This might include links to a new blog you like, a film you've recently been inspired by, or a news article about your favorite independent bookstore.

- **Personal, behind-the-scenes glimpses of your work, inspirations, or life.** Whether shown through the witty thoughts that come to your mind, the photos you snapped over the weekend, or the short QuickTime movies of your trip to the local flea market, these can tell readers a bit more about your real life.

- **Sneak peeks.** Your readers will love getting a peek into the ideas you're drumming up for a new column or the companies you're working with on a giveaway. So tell them about an upcoming giveaway in advance, or ask them for feedback on who or what they'd love to see featured on your site.

- **Communications with other businesses, bloggers, and people you admire.** Twitter is a two-way street, and the fun comes not only from what you say and share, but also from what you learn about others. Strangely enough, one of my closest friendships started with a conversation on Twitter that eventually led to our realizing more of our shared interests and becoming steadfast friends in real life.

One of the coolest things about Twitter is the instant feedback and interaction you get. If you're working on a project and need suggestions for inspiring graphic designers, all you have to do is ask. Or if you're in Portland for the weekend and need a restaurant recommendation, your Twitter followers can chime in if they have a great pick for you. When it comes to whom to follow, there are no rules. You also don't have to follow everyone who follows you or respond to every reply you get. While it's nice to show appreciation for people's suggestions after you ask for their feedback on a topic, you can tweet a general thanks to everyone if you don't have time to respond to each one personally. Also, try to keep things positive. No one wants to read a never-ending Debbie Downer rant. Those who tend to just vent about how much work they have to do or how many e-mails they're behind on, or complain about their clients, don't offer much to inspire others. So while you can certainly share your thoughts and struggles from time to time, remember that Twitter is not a place to air your dirty laundry.

OTHER SOCIAL MEDIA PLATFORMS

These days, many programs and applications—from Tumblr to Pinterest, Foodspotting to Foursquare—have a built-in social media aspect. Whether they are meant to share images, photos, experiences, or locations, these applications allow you to "follow" others, comment on images that have been uploaded, or "like" things that fellow users post—enhancing the experience and increasing your web of virtual connections. For example, as a photographer, having a Tumblr or Instagram account will offer readers a visual summary of your day-to-day life through pictures and give fans a more in-depth look into how you see the world. Or, if you're a food blogger, Foursquare or Foodspotting offers your followers an in-the-moment look at where you're eating. Any time you sign up for a new social networking tool, try to keep your username consistent across all tools (whether you use your blog name or your personal name), so that fans can more quickly find you in multiple places. More social networking tools spring up every day, so stay abreast of what's new and picking up speed, as it just might be one more tool you can add to your social networking arsenal.

LAUNCHED IN 1993, kate spade new york has evolved from a simple handbag line to a complete lifestyle brand. In 2010, the team behind kate spade new york began their efforts in social media to keep the brand in the forefront of the virtual conversation through the company's blog as well as its Twitter, Facebook, and Tumblr sites. Cecilia Liu is the digital marketing manager for kate spade new york, where she manages the company's social media strategies. I discussed with her the importance of connecting with customers—especially those that are bloggers—in a more direct, interactive, and playful format.

? *How does kate spade new york use social media outlets on a daily basis? And how do you use each differently to interact with customers?*

Facebook has been a great way to interact with our customers, because we receive so many product- and shopping-related questions there. We can use it to find out complaints customers may have as well as hear feedback on our products. We use Twitter as the voice of the "kate spade new york girl." The tweets tell us about what she's doing, what she's wearing, and the events she's attending when she's out and about in the city. In tandem with Twitter, we use Instagram to capture images of the moments she's living, and we share the kate spade new york lifestyle through these tweets, images, and check-ins through Foursquare. From a Vampire Weekend concert to a croissant from a local bakery, we show fans how she's living her interesting life, and we hope it inspires in turn.

On our Tumblr page and on our blog, Behind the Curtain, the kate spade new york lifestyle comes alive through visuals. Tumblr is like a living, constantly refreshing inspiration board and activity log, while on the blog, we show an in-depth look and the creative engine behind the scenes. We'll do profiles on those we partner with on special collections, and "how she wore it" shows celebrity and street style—which all enhance the feel of our brand and gets that image out there. We want to show how all that inspiration we derive from the world turns into what we create as a brand. We've also chronicled an archive of past store openings, events, and our partnerships with artists and illustrators. We have lots of components to our brand, which we try to keep updated regularly with interesting new content for our fans.

Do you find that one of these tools is more effective than others?

I really think it's the perfect storm to use a combination of them all. You have to figure out the best way to use these types of conversations to interact with your customer. Facebook, with the greatest audience of all our social channels, is our hub for all social activity. We use Twitter to keep up conversations and the "live stream" from the brand. We use Foursquare and Instagram more as complementary tools than primary vehicles, since they are a way of telling a more detailed story when used in conjunction with Twitter. Tumblr is our visual stream of consciousness. And all these channels drive back to the main Web site in some way. Before jumping into any new platform, we'll always consider how it'll work best for what we need.

How has being active in these social media outlets increased your customer base and loyalty?

It's definitely been a return in engagement. On Facebook, where customers act as a community, they feel more connected to our brand when they are part of the dialogue. Whether positive or negative, there's a level of customer engagement that we hadn't been able to create prior to being active in these social media outlets. On Twitter, we see lots of engagement when followers share inspiration, answer styling questions, or just tell us what they bought from our stores that weekend. It's a true two-way, authentic conversation. We're also constantly thinking about return on investment and how do you turn all these followers into sales. I think that's what every brand is

----->

trying to figure out, and I think the solution will be unique for different brands and their customers. We've amassed more than 350,000 fans on Facebook and 100,000 followers on Twitter—the sheer size of that social community and their engagement levels is crucial to us in cultivating a real and authentic relationship with as many customers and potential customers and fans as we can.

What's the value of bloggers to your brand and business?

Bloggers are an essential part of the network with brands like kate spade new york. They offer an unbiased viewpoint to their audience in fashion, graphic design, or whatever their niche is. Every blogger we choose to work with has their own take on style, and because their audience follows them for what they like, it's usually very authentic. We love that they have a voice that is unbiased and truly their own, so we love seeing our products on their blogs because it means they deem our brand a good fit for their readers. A lot of our partnerships come from the girls who have approached us to say they personally love kate spade new york, and as long as we feel their blog and brand fits with our aesthetic—color, charm, wit, personality, and a bit of cheekiness—we're totally open to exploring a collaboration.

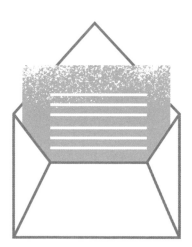

CONFERENCES

In the same way that a local meet-up helps you connect face-to-face, blog conferences do this on a larger, nationwide scale. In addition to allowing you to meet fellow bloggers from all over the country, conferences also offer workshops on various blogging topics, like food photography or monetizing your blog. It's a fun way to get more tips on how to grow your blog while meeting others at the same time. There are plenty of blogging conferences out there, including BlogHer, Altitude Design Summit, and BlogWorld (see Resources). Some are more general and appeal to any type of blogger, while others are more focused on topics such as design, lifestyle, motherhood, or food. When researching which would be the best to attend, it's nice to

> You might feel less intimidated and more comfortable striking up conversations when the number of attendees is more accessible.

start with a smaller conference that has a few hundred people in attendance instead of a few thousand. You might feel less intimidated and more comfortable striking up conversations when the number of attendees is more accessible. Conferences covering topics that you're interested in and that focus on your niche will also be beneficial for meeting others with similar interests and learning the tips and skills you may need help with. Be sure to carry business cards with you so that the end of any conversation can be punctuated with a leave-behind to remind fellow bloggers where to find you or how to stay in touch.

BLOGGER, ENTREPRENEUR, AND MOM of six, Gabrielle Blair came up with the idea for Altitude Design Summit with her sisters in 2009 while on vacation in Mexico. Her sisters—Jordan Ferney, Sara Urquhart, and Liz Stanley—were also design and lifestyle bloggers, who felt there wasn't a conference for bloggers in their niche. Gabrielle had been going to blogging conferences for years, but they were mom-focused and didn't emphasize the design aspect that she covered on her blog Design Mom. The idea grew, and the first Altitude Design Summit in Salt Lake City, Utah—with 150 attendees and 50 speakers—became reality in January 2010.

As Gabrielle and her co-founder/sister Sara intended, the conference focused on the needs of design and lifestyle bloggers by hosting a variety of events, panels, and workshops that would appeal to them all. They know that networking is not easy for everyone, so the ladies behind the conference make an effort to keep it approachable with limited-size classes and chances to meet and hang out with fellow bloggers at social events. Because blogging is often a solo activity with a lack of real-life interaction, Gabrielle emphasizes how important it is to not only network virtually but also to make real-life connections with fellow bloggers in person.

? *What types of panelists speak at Altitude Design Summit? And what are the various topics covered?*

We started by focusing on lifestyle and design blogs, because those are the people that we know, read, connect with, and whom we could ask to speak and help out. So our speakers, most of whom are bloggers, run the gamut from design to fashion, food, home décor, personal, and lifestyle.

As a blogger, you need to be able to write, photograph, and prep your posts. Nowadays, you might also need some technical programming abilities,

PR skills, and marketing savvy, so we want to be able to provide speakers and workshops to guide you through all of that. Also, we have to adapt as we see trends emerging and interest from our attendees in new areas. For example, after our first year, we saw more interest in photography, so we added more photographers as panelists and photography workshops the following year. And, since social media is an important part of what we want to teach bloggers about, we have to keep updating our classes as social media changes. So we're constantly watching to see what's new and what will be most relevant to the bloggers who attend each year.

? *What types of bloggers attend the conference, and why do you think they come?*

We have a wide range of attendees. Some are professional bloggers who are doing it for a living and have let another career go, and some are novices to blogging. We also have businesses and traditional media attending, as well as blog readers who are simply big fans and come to the conference to meet their favorite bloggers in real life.

The nature of blogs is very personal, and a blog is usually a good reflection of what's happening in people's lives. So people come to hone their skills, make real-life connections, and renew friendships.

? *Why do you think it's important for bloggers to network and attend conferences?*

When I think back on my life and career when I was in New York and working as an art director in an ad agency, I had people to bounce ideas off of, water cooler conversations, and regular human interaction. When you decide to blog, you're on your own in your home, and all of that co-worker support disappears. For most bloggers, they're not working in a studio space with others. So when you go to a conference, you get a better sense of what the blogging community is like. Once you meet someone in person, you're able to make a much stronger connection, which gives you a stronger sense of

- - - - - →

community. So when you're brainstorming and need advice or feedback, you can more easily reach out to someone you've met in person, like you would a co-worker or a business partner. I think that everyone finds it so comforting to see that other bloggers are real people. Also, most women tend to want to connect offline, and conferences are a great way to do that. You also get to write it off as a work expense!

What would you suggest to someone who wants to attend a blogger conference but doesn't know anyone attending or is scared of showing up alone?

Do some outreach ahead of time, even if it's just a tweet or an e-mail to bloggers you're friendly with or whose blogs you read. Tell them you're nervous about going and that you don't really know anyone, and ask them to meet you at the registration desk. Chances are, you'll find someone who's feeling the same way!

Also, try to find someone attending to share a hotel room with. In addition to being able to share some of the expenses, now you've got a buddy that you can leave the room with and walk down to the events with so you're not alone. Even if that person doesn't turn into your best friend, you automatically have someone to have dinner, attend events, or explore the city with during your free time.

ACCEPTING Submissions

Depending on the type of blog you have, part of your growing community and the content for your blog may include the people and businesses that you feature. You may notice various companies, artists, and PR reps start to e-mail you products or services they offer that they'd love you to blog about. Or maybe a reader has come up with a great DIY project that they'd like to share and hope you'll feature. It's always flattering when you receive e-mails like these because it means that others are taking note of and enjoying what you're putting out there. As your readership grows, it may be necessary to manage the onslaught of submission e-mails. One way to do this is to list your submission criteria on your home page or contact page. You can state what types of things you post about, if you take reader submissions, what to include in a submission e-mail (like small jpegs, under 100K in size, of the project or product and a link to their Web site), and when they should expect to hear back from you. That way you avoid getting e-mails about baby toys if you never post about kids' products, and people know that if you haven't responded within a week it's likely you felt the product wasn't the best fit for your blog content. Also, if your blog concept is heavily based on reader submissions, you'll want to be as clear as possible about your requirements in order to receive the entries that best fit your aesthetic or concept. Finally, you can set your e-mail filters to scan subject lines with the word "submission" and file these into one folder so that you can tackle all your submission e-mails at once.

GIVING *Credit*

Because blogging is still a fairly new phenomenon, with few standard rules and regulations, it is often considered to be the Wild West of new media. When it comes to the ethics and etiquette of blogging, there aren't very many doctrines. Because it's so easy to pull an image off the Internet and no

{ Because blogging is still a fairly new phenomenon, with few standard rules and regulations, it is often considered to be the Wild West of new media. }

copyright police to immediately stop you, many people are unaware that it's necessary to obtain permission from and then credit the sources (the photographer, illustrator, artist, or company) of any images you use online that you haven't created yourself. For example, the images you see in magazines or ads may belong to either the photographer or the publisher. So always get permission first, give credit where credit is due, and make sure you're giving props to the people or companies responsible for the images you feature.

While many people are appreciative of any business or traffic you send their way and do not require permission in advance, it's always better to err on the side of caution and ask for permission instead of simply linking credits. If you don't know where an image came from, you can check TinEye's Web site (see Resources), which serves as a reverse image search engine, and find out where an image originally came from. Typically, you'll want to avoid posting any images without permission from newspapers, magazines, or any other artist or creative person whose work is not promotional in nature.

PRODUCT CREDIT

Whenever you feature a product on your site and pull an image for it from another Web site, a simple product credit should name the item and store, and provide a link to where you can buy it. In addition, if you make your product credit clear (by using the specific store and product names in your hyperlinks), you can even improve your blog's search engine results. For example: "Spoonflower mod dot canvas fabric" (all underlined words would be hyperlinks to those sources).

Even if you have a journal-style blog and take your own photos, you can note your sources. Someone may love the dress you're wearing or the cocktail glasses you used in a recipe and inquire about them, so it's helpful to state an item's origins at the bottom of your post. Also indicate if any items were gifts from companies. For example: "Rosanna plates, glasses courtesy of Fishes Eddy, Murray's sharp cheddar cheese."

MULTIPLE PRODUCT CREDIT

If you create a product roundup or montage, you need to make clear which credit is for which product or image. You can do this by adding numbers or labels to your layout or by making sure products are listed in a certain orientation (like clockwise) so readers can easily find the links for each. Then cite the corresponding credits; for example:

"1. Hui Hui necklace, 2. Welcome wagon/bag by Laurel Broughton, 3. Nesting tables from Anthropologie, 4. Dinner plate from Terrain, 5. World map from The Future Mapping Company" or "Clockwise: Hui Hui necklace; welcome wagon/bag by Laurel Broughton; nesting tables from Anthropologie; dinner plate from Terrain; world map from The Future Mapping Company."

PHOTO CREDIT

If you place an image that doesn't belong to you in a post, you should credit the photographer and publication, as they own the rights to it. However, as a courtesy, you can also credit the team, such as the model and hair or makeup artist, or the prop stylist. For example:

"Photography by Gilles Bensimon and styling by Rebecca Thuss for *Elle Decor*, March 2009."

Before you pull any image from a site, you should check if the photographer has a policy regarding taking images from his or her site. A photographer may require you to obtain permission before posting the image. Also, if there is a watermark on the photo, removing it is a violation of the artist's copyright and must not be done. In the end, a photographer's work should only be posted if you receive permission and clearly credit him or her.

LINK LOVE

Show appreciation for your fellow bloggers by giving them credit if you're posting about a topic or company that you originally found through their site. A simple note and a link to their blog at the bottom of your post gives them props for inspiring you. For example, "West Elm blanket via DesignLoveFest."

Or if a reader or fellow blogger e-mailed you about something they thought you'd want to post about, mention it in your post. For example: "Milk crates from Three Potato Four. Thanks, Sally!"

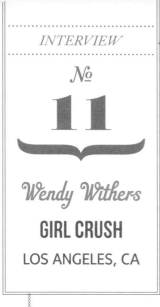

WENDY WITHERS came up with the idea for her blog, Girl Crush, when she was pregnant with her first son in 2007. At the time, she was a successful art producer and photo editor with more than eighteen years under her belt and was concerned about how she'd transition from being a full-time professional to a full-time mother. She found inspiration on how to juggle both sides by learning from other women and working moms—and she loved the idea of sharing their stories in a blog. She marinated on the concept for a couple of years, and once her "mom fog" lifted after having her second son, she started Girl Crush in 2011 to share women's stories, both the highs and lows of their lives and careers and everything in between.

? *Who do you feature on your blog?*

I feature women from all over the world, though most are based in the United States. I truly believe that we all have something interesting to say and are all inspirational in some way. I try to feature a range of women, some of whom are mothers, as well as those who are not. They cover fields such as dance, medicine, architecture, food, construction, and art. I've even featured a firefighter and an astronaut.

? *How much time do you spend blogging? And how do you carve out the time in addition to being a mom?*

Blogging often feels like a full-time job because I love it so much. I probably spend thirty hours per week on my blog, including researching who I'll feature next, contacting them, getting the images and story together, and then constructing the actual post. I update my blog once a week with a new interview. As a full-time mom, I blog whenever I can, finding little pockets of free time throughout the week. I haven't had consistent help with the boys, so whenever I do have help, I grab the computer and go. I never know when I'm going to become inspired, or receive a lead for a story, so not having a schedule is working for me at the moment.

Did you know much about starting a blog when you began? How did you build it and make it come together technically?

I knew absolutely nothing about starting a blog when I began. I'm extremely tech deficient. I started with a free blogging account, but it drove me crazy with all the HTML, so I moved to WordPress, which I found to be much more intuitive. I used a free template in the beginning as I was figuring out the content of my blog. Once I had a more defined concept and it was growing, I started thinking about having a logo and site designed. I worked with a friend who's a Web designer to create my logo, design my site, and help me realize my vision.

How do you select photos and write the interviews?

Initially, I thought I'd shoot photos of the subjects myself, but I soon realized that would be impossible, since many of the profiled women live far from me. So the subjects of the story provide the photos, giving each story its own unique flavor. Most of the women's stories are told through a Q&A, and then I write an introduction based on their unique narrative. I recently interviewed an artist and wrote the introduction based on how I imagined it might be to spend a vacation inside her head, because her work is so beautiful and lively. I don't have any formal writing experience, so the words come out organically.

How has your blog helped you with motherhood while being at home with the kids?

Girl Crush has been a tremendous help in terms of guiding me through motherhood and meeting smart, interesting people that help me stay connected with the world while being a stay-at-home mom. Before I started my blog,

- - - - - →

I was very concerned about my career and how I would find something for myself to do after leaving my job. It's made me a better mother and has been a huge motivating factor in my life. Every single woman I feature inspires and empowers me to appreciate my life and make the most out of Girl Crush.

I feel very fortunate that people allow me to share and curate their personal journeys. With each story I gain more momentum and the desire to share more stories about women and what they do in their lives. It inspires the way that I shape my own life and that of my family. I would love to see this series become a book, especially to inspire young girls, women stuck in a rut, women in transition, and just women in general. I think we all have something to learn from one another.

COMMENTING 101

Comments allow you to know what readers have to say in response to the content you're bringing to them. It gives your audience a place to interact with you and with one another. While it's also a good idea to list your e-mail address on your blog so that followers can contact you, most readers will respond to your content via comments rather than e-mail you directly. When your blog is fresh and new, you'll probably sit there, eager for your first comment to appear. A comment from a complete stranger can be an exciting experience and shows you that people are slowly, but surely, finding your little Web home. As your site grows, the number of comments you receive will also grow, and you'll find that you can start to track the growth of your site by the increased number of comments you get daily. So, remember to engage your readers and ask them questions in your posts every so often that elicit their interaction and encourage them to add to the conversation.

MODERATING OR REMOVING COMMENTS

Some people feel as though readers should be able to say anything they want in any public space, like a blog. If you find yourself with comments that are less than ideal, you can choose to moderate comments, but remember not to remove comments simply because they are negative. Think carefully before removing any comments. If it's a justified opinion, your blog may be attacked further for overly censoring your comments. Even negative comments are a part of the conversation you're creating (see more on negative comments on page 100).

While some may feel strongly about their First Amendment rights, you have the right to try to keep your space on the Internet as positive as possible. One way to help steer comments toward the positive and constructive is by adding a guideline that appears in every comment section; for example: "The Oh Joy! blog reserve the right to remove comments that are self-promotional, rude, personal attacks, or not contributing to the topic at hand." This can set the tone for your blog and hopefully gives readers a bit of protocol when commenting.

CLOSING COMMENTS

Closing comments after a certain amount of time is usually best for giveaways or contests. If readers need to leave a comment to enter your contest, specify how long entries can be posted, and know that you'll eventually have to close comments when that deadline comes to an end. Or if some pages on your site are meant to be more informational (like an FAQ or About page), you may choose to close comments since it's not a typical post where a conversation would take place.

RESPONDING TO COMMENTS

Responding to comments is a great way to build your following and show readers that you are active in the conversation surrounding your blog's content. You don't need to respond to every comment, but if a reader asks a question about a post, you should either respond to that reader directly through e-mail, by commenting in the post, or both. It's possible that if someone asks where you found that neon pink thread used to make your own oven mitts, others might be wondering the same thing as well. If readers are congratulating you on your recent news, like a big project you completed with a dream client or the recent birth of your baby, you may get a double dose of congratulatory comments. Depending on how much time you can dedicate to it, you can e-mail a response to each reader with a simple "thank you!" or post an all-encompassing message acknowledging all your readers' kind words. They'll be delighted to hear from you and appreciate that you took the time to respond. While you may find yourself overwhelmed with keeping up with this as your site grows, remember that it's the readers who visit regularly that are helping to grow your blog, so always do your best to thank them by answering their questions and keeping the flow of dialogue going.

NEGATIVE COMMENTS

At some point in your blogging lifetime, someone will say something inappropriate or mean on your blog or even in an e-mail to you. As outraged or hurt as that may make you, the best thing to do is step back and look at the message for what it is and not the emotions that may naturally pour out of you. Consider what the comment is saying, and be open to any constructive criticism offered. If the comment is suggesting something you could improve upon, send the commenter an e-mail stating your appreciation for bringing the issue to light. Or if the statement was based on a mistake you made, be ready to apologize for it and show that you're not perfect. When dealing with negative comments, here are a few things to consider:

- **Is it a misunderstanding?** Perhaps you posted an image with monochromatic portraits of various people and labeled the post "Black and White." Maybe someone read that as a racial statement and left a comment in response. Instead, you simply meant it as a description of the black-and-white film used, not the people in the image. If their response is based on something that was unclear or could be misconstrued, clarify the post and your intentions to the reader, as well as in the Comments section of your blog so that other readers can learn from the update as well.

Is the comment a negative criticism or a personal attack on a topic you've posted? If a reader simply doesn't like the piece of art you posted or doesn't think the quality is up to par, that comment is their personal opinion, not a personal attack on the artist. However, if the comment seems to come from a nonconstructive and personal place, then you can consider removing it. When someone is personally attacking someone you've chosen to feature on your blog, you may choose not to subject that person to unnecessary roughness when they didn't ask for it.

Is it a personal attack on you? Some comments may simply say, "I don't like your blog" or "You suck!" If that's the case, the reader should spend their time elsewhere. They are usually just being mean for the sake of it. Stylist Emily Henderson (who is profiled on page 115) often repeats a quote by Bill Cosby when dealing with mean comments on her blog: "I don't know what the key to success is. But the key to failure is trying to impress everybody." It's helpful to remind yourself not to take it personally and that you can't be everything to everyone. These negative Nellies probably make up a tiny percentage of the people who read and love what you have to say. These types of comments can be ignored, and if you choose to leave them up, chances are that your loyal readers will stand by your side and defend you from the person.

While you can certainly choose to have a comment-free blog altogether, remember that comments help to build community and promote conversations among the like-minded, creative people you're attracting to your site. Most people are kind and encouraging, so always pay attention to the positive conversations happening on your blog, and let those be the ones that encourage you to keep sharing your story with others.

CHAPTER 05

{ MAKING YOUR BLOG *a* BUSINESS }

If you're thinking of generating income through your blog, likely through ads, that means that your site will become a business and be subject to taxes and regulations. This chapter will guide you through the basics of turning your blog into a business, including planning the finances, filing the proper paperwork, protecting and copyrighting your work, and creating a business plan for future growth. You'll find that various parts of this chapter will apply to you at different stages in your blogging path, so take each step as it comes and remind yourself that as serious as some of it may sound, these steps are all signs that your blog is growing and doing well.

BUSINESS *Essentials*

Whether you've banked $100 or $10,000, once your blog is earning any sort of income, there are things you'll need to consider to make your new blog official, like getting a business license, a business bank account, and possibly trademarking your blog's name. You'll also have to think about protective measures such as health insurance and your legal structure. Following are the basic necessities for getting your blog established as a legitimate business.

FICTITIOUS BUSINESS NAME

The name of your blog can, of course, be the name of your business. Unless your blog uses your legal name, you'll need to register a fictitious business name (also known as a DBA—"Doing Business As"—in the United States, or T/A—"Trading As"—in the United Kingdom) so that you can apply for various licenses, get a business bank account, and be paid or make payments under that name. Luckily, it's a pretty easy and inexpensive step. Depending on your location, a DBA can be filed either through the Secretary of State or your county clerk's office. Two businesses in the same state or county cannot have the same name, so this is what the appropriate agency will be checking for when you perform an initial search in their database. If the name is free and clear, you'll submit a form, pay the fee, and possibly have to publish a notice in your local newspaper before it can be finalized.

BUSINESS LICENSE

Depending on where you live, you may be required to apply for a license to officially conduct business and possibly need a separate home occupation business license to run your business from home. The U.S. Small Business Administration can give you guidelines for what you need based on your state and where you plan to work. Along with your local chamber of commerce, you can find out the type of license you'll need, how to go about applying for it, and what fees are involved. Your business license needs to be displayed in your workspace and will be necessary to open a business bank account.

TRADEMARK

If you want to have complete ownership of the name of your blog through-out the United States (not just your state), you'll have to file a trademark. A trademark is a name, word, phrase, logo, symbol, image, or a combination of these elements. To register a trademark and protect your name from being used by others, you have to go through the U.S. Patent and Trademark Office (USPTO; see Resources) to do a search and make sure the name is available for use. If the name you've chosen is available, you can file an application for use of the mark. The waiting time for a trademark can range from a few months to more than a year, depending on the reason for filing and any legal issues that may arise. If you prefer to leave the legal stuff to the experts, a small-business lawyer can also take care of filing your trademark.

BUSINESS BANK ACCOUNT

For tax purposes, you'll want to keep any income made on your blog or any money spent on it separate from your personal finances. Opening up a business bank account will keep your blog finances independent of your personal finances and make it much easier to file taxes. To open a business

> Opening up a business bank account will keep your blog finances independent of your personal finances and make it much easier to file taxes.

bank account, you'll need to show the bank your fictitious name statement (if you're using a DBA) along with your business license. While you're at it, open a business savings account as well so that you can deposit a portion of every check you receive. It's always best to put those tax pennies aside instead of trying to come up with your full tax payment in one lump sum at the end of the year.

FEDERAL TAX ID

If your blog is a partnership or you have (or plan to have) employees, you'll need to apply for a federal tax ID number, also known as an employer identification number (EIN). Otherwise, as a solo blogger, your individual social security number is sufficient for filing taxes. Having an EIN is also helpful when companies who advertise with you require you to fill out a W-9 form (a taxpayer identification form, which is often required before a sponsor or client can pay you). By having an EIN, you can fill out the paperwork they need without giving them your personal social security number. The IRS Web site (IRS.gov) can give you more details on how to go about applying for your EIN.

YOUR LEGAL STRUCTURE

Every legal structure has its own set of pros and cons. Many bloggers automatically choose a sole proprietorship as their legal structure, since it's the easiest to do when working solo. However, a C-Corporation, S-Corporation, or Limited Liability Corporation may be options to consider as well. Each one has its own set of tax and asset protection benefits (in case you are sued). You can learn more about the differences between them on the Small Business Administration's Web site (sba.gov), or you can turn to a small-business accountant or lawyer for additional guidance.

HEALTH INSURANCE

We often take it for granted, but health insurance is essential to stay protected when sickness or emergencies arise. If you're no longer at your full-time job, are unable to use the COBRA (Consolidated Omnibus Budget Reconciliation Act) plan, which extends the coverage you had at a past job, or don't have a partner whose insurance will cover you, there are many health coverage plans out there to satisfy your needs and budget. Your state insurance department can give you a list of health insurance options in your area so you can compare plans and choose what's best for your needs.

Protecting YOUR WORK

Part of becoming a more established blogger includes taking some protective measures to prevent others from lifting your content. Following are some safeguards you should implement when it comes to protecting your blog.

Courtesy Line. It helps to add a courtesy line to the bottom of your blog that lets others know how you conduct business and how you hope they will, too. It largely serves as a deterrent (similar to placing a home alarm sign outside your house). For example, mine says:

> All layouts and graphics on this blog are created solely for the Oh Joy! blog. I enjoy sharing information, and love when others enjoy my finds enough to post the links on their own sites. However, I ask that you do not use my exact layouts or designs without permission or without noting its origins on your post. Oh Joy!® is a registered trademark of Nantaka Joy®, Inc. All rights reserved.

Time Stamp. You have to your advantage the time that your blog existed prior to a blog that copied you, and can prove that the content existed on your site initially before being copied. You can check to see if your content has been duplicated by using a Web site like Copyscape. Similar to an Internet search, after pasting your URL into a search box, Copyscape will search the Web for any copies of your content that were used in other places. You can also install a program like Tynt, which helps protect your content by embedding a code with your URL into any text or images that someone attempts to copy and paste from your site (see Resources).

Creative Commons License. Creative Commons serves as a way to support and protect the online work of creatives like photographers, artists, and bloggers. You can place on your blog the simple and standardized text and icons, which notify users of the copyright permissions of your creative work. By choosing from a set of six licenses, you can tell others which part of your work they can and can't use, publish, print, or distribute.

Copyright. Copyright is a set of exclusive rights granted to the author of an original work. The original work can include text, paintings, photographs, sound recordings, and motion pictures that you've created for your blog. The good news is that you have the Berne Convention on your side. This is a treaty that states that once your content has been published on the Internet, it's automatically copyrighted, and you are the copyright holder. The United States has signed this treaty with only certain countries, so if an infringer is in a country that has signed the treaty with the United States (and you live in the U.S.), this treaty would be in your favor. Be sure to add a line on your blog stating the current year and the copyright holder (that's you!) at the bottom of your site. Depending on the nature of your specific blog content, you should check with a lawyer to see if you should also have your blog copyrighted through the U.S. Copyright Office as an added protective measure.

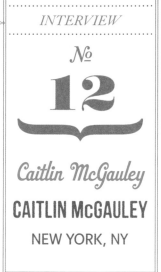

"THE WHOLE REASON I have an illustration career is because of my blog," says illustrator and blogger Caitlin McGauley. After enrolling in Syracuse University as an illustration major, she worried that she'd never get a job as an illustrator, so she switched to advertising design—which seemed like a more practical major with more job options. However, Caitlin continued to take electives in surface pattern design so that she could still practice her love of illustration. After graduation, Caitlin landed a job at Ralph Lauren as a bedding textile designer but still craved her true passion and sought freelance illustration work on the side. Unfortunately, her desire was met by many rejections from illustration representatives, who said they liked her work but felt that she didn't have a specific voice. Looking to develop her style and aesthetic and show that she had something interesting to offer, Caitlin started her self-titled blog in 2008. These days, she showcases colorful watercolor illustrations of things such as the gelato she just ate, the espadrilles she's coveting, or a nook in her bedroom she just spruced up—all in the signature style that she developed through her blog. This didn't go without notice—publishing her artwork on her blog has brought Caitlin clients such as online Lonny Magazine, kate spade new york, and Hermès. Now, Caitlin has the career she has always wanted and confidence in her style and work due to the time she put into nurturing her talent through her blog.

How long did it take for you to develop your style? And how did your blog help you do that?

By my fourth or fifth post. I did a small painting of Rizzoli, my favorite bookstore in New York City. I had always put these heavy black outlines on my watercolor illustrations because they never looked finished to me without them. But this painting was just a loose watercolor, with no lines to define it or to give it a stylized look, and I just decided to paint more loosely at that

- - - - - →

point. When it comes to watercolor, practice and experimentation are really important, so a blog can be a great forum to get yourself to paint regularly. Feedback from readers is so valuable. I am so grateful and excited to get comments, and it really encourages me to keep going.

? *What career opportunities have come to you because of your blog?*

I had started my blog while I was still working full-time at Ralph Lauren. Before starting Lonny Magazine, Michelle Adams (the editor in chief) had her own blog, which I liked and would comment on. From one of my comments, she went to my blog and really liked my style and asked me to do the illustrations for Lonny. After we discussed it, she had me on board before the magazine launched. One assignment for Lonny was an illustration of the kate spade new york store in New York. From that, kate spade new york asked me to illustrate artwork for dishes and other prints they wanted to sell. And after an article about Lonny in *Vanity Fair* (where they mentioned me as their illustrator), Hermès contacted me to see if I'd paint portraits of people at their events—like a cooler version of the caricatures they do at the circus! Then DailyCandy did a video on me about being an artist who did commissions and portraits, so I started getting inquiries from people (not just businesses) to paint a scene of their house or someone's favorite pair of shoes. It was just one great thing that led to another.

? *Was it difficult at first to put your work out there, since it was still a work in progress of sorts?*

It was not difficult to put my work out there because I didn't have any readers at first! Even though I am more confident with my style now, I always ask myself, Who will be reading this and is the story interesting enough to tell? So I definitely put more thought into my posts now. The initial response was slow going, but it just makes me appreciate all of the feedback I get now and the work that it took to get to this point. I was posting more in the beginning than I am now, because back then I just had my full-time job and the blog to work on.

How long does it take you to create your drawn blog posts?

If I have a concept in mind, it usually takes about an hour to draw it, scan it, and post it. I don't sketch things in advance. I make a mental note of things I want to paint. Sometimes I can go home and paint it from memory, or—say it was a pair of shoes I'm lusting after—I might look them up online to get a better image to paint from. I often love the watercolor illustrations I do for my blog more than those I do for clients, because they're more natural and less thought out.

When did you decide to freelance full-time?

I was still at Ralph Lauren as a bedding textile designer when this was all happening, and I was working around the clock. In early 2011, I started thinking about going full-time with my freelance work when I was pregnant with my first baby. I knew I couldn't work full-time, freelance on the side, and have a baby, so I left my job because I had enough freelance work that I could really make a go of it.

You sell some of your work as prints. Why did you start your print shop?

I was getting a lot of inquiries about prints from readers. It's probably the most common e-mail request I get. When developing the four prints I started with, I wanted to show a variety of subjects—a room/décor scene and a fashion girl, because those were the types of things readers requested, and then butterflies and necklaces, because those were objects that I liked. My goal is to change the prints I offer every couple months, maybe with something specific to the season each time.

How has blogging enhanced your skills and talent as an illustrator?

It's definitely given me a lot more confidence and practice in my art. I can look back on my work and see how much easier it has gotten for me to create new images, how much less time it takes than before, and how much better it looks than it used to. It's also helped me to understand what people like and respond to best from the comments I've received.

----->

Also, the people I've met in the blogging community have really been incredible. Michelle and Patrick from Lonny really put me on the map. I'm so appreciative of the people who leave me comments and how they care about what's going on in my life. The overall connection with people has been the best part of all of this.

? *What tips do you have for someone who wants to use a blog to develop their style and talent?*

I cannot stress enough that a blog is the best way to develop a style. Sometimes people e-mail me and ask about technique or how to achieve a certain look with watercolor. I always say the same thing—it just takes a ton of practice! You can't help but develop a style, or get better at your style, if you have the discipline to paint nearly every day.

Financing YOUR BLOG BUSINESS

A huge benefit of blogging is that you don't need a whole lot of capital to start. Aside from a possible monthly fee for your blog host and the cost of a computer (which you may already have), overhead is usually low, especially if you're blogging from home. However, if you're at a point where you've turned into an income-earning professional blogger, you'll need to consider how you'll live off this income (see more about becoming a full-time blogger in chapter 7).

For any expenses you incur for your blog, using cash you have in the bank is ideal. However, you can consider using credit cards to help cover some blogging expenses as long as they are used with caution! As appealing as a 0 percent APR credit card may be now, there are often hidden fees that pop up at some point down the road. Since your blog may not earn income right away or even for a few years, be careful when getting spend-happy. Look into refurbished scanners, cameras, or other blogger gear on Craigslist or a trusted equipment shop, and buy these supplies and tools only when you really need them and they're essential for increasing the quality of your blogging abilities. Work from home (or a local café with Wi-Fi) for as long as you can to save on expenses before considering a shared studio space. Also, consider trading or bartering with those skilled in other areas. You could call upon a graphic designer to design a banner for you in exchange for ad space or ask a photographer to take your head shot for your About page, and in return you'll link to their site when the photo is featured.

RECORD KEEPING and TAXES

Once your blog is a business, you'll want to track two very important things—your income and your expenses. Using programs like Excel, Quicken, or QuickBooks will help you log every check or payment you receive. As soon as you receive a payment, be sure to record the date, the company who paid you, and the amount received. Try not to let the records build up, as it's much easier to record a check or PayPal payment each time it comes through (or at least once a month) than have to spend days logging a pile of invoices at the end of the year. The great thing about keeping an up-to-date account of your blog income and expenses is that you can track how much you're making each month and start to see your potential earning power. Also, when you're ready to tackle your taxes, you'll be ready to go! At the end of every tax year, the IRS requires any companies that have paid you more than $600 that year to fill out a 1099 form and send you a copy by January 31 after the completed tax year. Make sure to match these statements up with your records, as you'll need to include copies of each one for your accountant.

If you're a self-employed blogger, filing taxes won't be just a yearly occurrence anymore. When your blog earns a profit of more than $1,000 for the year, the IRS requires you to pay state and federal taxes quarterly. Typically, you'll need to pay anywhere from 25 to 48 percent of your income in taxes, depending on how much you're earning per year. Any time you receive a payment, it's best to put part of those funds into your business savings account so that the money isn't touched until your tax payments are due. You may have to file quarterly (and potentially make payments each quarter)—on

April 15, June 15, October 15, and January 15—as an estimate of what you will owe at year-end. While you can certainly tackle this on your own with the help of the IRS Web site (irs.gov), you may choose to seek the help of an accountant to get you on track and explain all the details to you in layman's terms if you're not feeling savvy in this area.

EXPENSE IT!

As a business, you should begin to take advantage of any items that can be considered a business expense to help reduce your taxable income. Any materials or tools you used or trips you took in order to create and compose your blog posts can now be counted as expenses and should be logged and submitted to your accountant quarterly. Obvious business expenses include your computer, scanner, camera, and any software (like Photoshop) that you use to create your posts. But you can also expense items like the baking supplies you used to make a recipe, the new beauty products you bought to review and share with readers, any business lunches you had with advertisers or clients, and your hotel stays for blogging conferences.

Since most blogging is done from the comfort of your own home, a portion of your home bills (including rent and utilities) can be deducted if that space is dedicated to blogging. So your dining room table or your living room doesn't count if the rest of your family uses that area of the house for meals or recreation. If you do have a room you use solely for blogging, then you can calculate the percentage of space it occupies within the full square footage of your home. For example, if your blogging office is one-fifth the square footage of your home, then one-fifth of your expenses such as rent, Internet, and electricity can be deducted and accounted for when filing your taxes. Now, this doesn't mean that you should take advantage of this tax deduction and expense everything in your life. If you appear to have too many expenses that overlap into personal territory, that can be a red flag for the IRS, so think carefully about what is a true business expense.

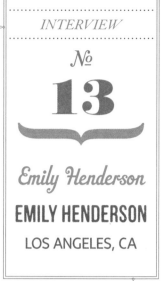

IT STARTED with just a dozen blog posts, but these triggered the events that would lead to the launch of Emily Henderson's own show on HGTV. Emily began her career in 2001 as a prop stylist working on sets in New York and Los Angeles, styling food, fashion, and still-life scenes for advertising and editorial clients like Target, West Elm, Martha Stewart Living Omnimedia, *InStyle*, and *Domino*. She started her blog, The Brass Petal, in early 2010, just a month shy of auditioning for the second season of *Design Star*, an HGTV competitive reality show. The support she received from blog readers gave her the confidence to try out for *Design Star*, which she won, leading to the launch of her own show, *Secrets from a Stylist*, on HGTV in 2011. Punctuated by her quirky personality and style of writing, her newest self-titled blog, Emily Henderson, lets her continue to connect with fans and viewers by giving them a behind-the-scenes look at her work and process and also lets her share personal experiences from her Mormon upbringing.

? *In the beginning, how did blogging change your work as a stylist?*

It was the first time I felt like I was interesting to other people. When you're working on shoots, you're not always credited for styling, or the credit is so minor. Oftentimes, people didn't understand what I really did or if I was any good at it. Once I blogged, I got instant positive feedback about my work, which gave me more validation and confidence. For some reason, people related to me, and in a good way. After seeing that type of feedback, I gained more confidence to go on *Design Star* . . . and then you know the rest!

? *Why should someone start a blog?*

I think that people often feel intimidated and feel like they might not be as accomplished in their field as others to justify having their own blog. It's okay if you're still learning your craft or you're not exactly where you want to be

- - - - - →

yet—you still have something to offer. I started my blog because I knew I had something to show people about the world of styling, and I just had to put myself out there. You have nothing to lose.

You started your blog before you went on the second season of Design Star, *and blogged throughout the entire season once it aired. How do you think that helped you interact with people watching the show?*

My blog helped me connect with other bloggers and readers, because when they watched the show, they felt like I was one of them (having known me from my blog prior to being on the show). I felt like I had an advantage over the contestants that didn't have blogs, because fans and viewers got to hear about my real feelings and what really happened on each episode from my point of view. Even though fans had no control over who won (and it was the judges' choice in the end), it showed the humanity of what it's like to be on a reality show, the constraints of each challenge, and my perspective throughout. People empathized with me when they knew more about the process.

You write in a very quirky, stream-of-consciousness manner and also share bits of your former Mormon lifestyle. Why did you choose to stay casual in your tone of voice and share this part of your life?

I knew I wouldn't blog if it wasn't easy, and writing the way you talk is easier than trying to be super-formal or structured. It would be forced if I didn't write that way. As for the Mormon posts, it's undeniable that what I do is a direct result of having grown up Mormon. Coming from a big family with six kids, crafting and canning in everyday life, and learning to be so resourceful at a young age really makes for pretty creative adults. One of my most popular posts is about why there are so many Mormons or former Mormons who are design bloggers, crafters, and work at Martha Stewart! Readers enjoy hearing about it, because either they know nothing about the religion or they're Mormon and like that I'm talking about it in a positive way.

CREATING A *Business Plan*

If your blog is gaining momentum and especially if it's growing quicker than you expected, that's incredible news, and means that you're obviously doing something right. If you find yourself with new opportunities knocking on your door from companies who want to work with you, establishing a business plan is a great way to come across as a professional blogger. It could also help you gain respect if you're looking to collaborate with another company, seek additional funding, or even someday sell your blog. A business plan essentially outlines your goals and what you'd need logistically and financially to maintain and take your blog business to the next level. The five major components of a basic business plan include:

1 A mission statement, describing the focus of your blog, your goals for it, and why it's of value to readers.

2 Background information, giving more insight into who you are. You should mention if you had previous professional experience in the industry, or if you or your blog received any notable awards or press.

3 A list of capabilities, indicating what types of ads you can offer potential sponsors, articles you can write for other blogs or magazines, benefits future investors might receive, or any strong concepts you have for book publishers. This part of the business plan should be tweaked depending on whom you're looking to reach or attract.

4 A market analysis, discussing any blog competition in your specific genre. This should state why you stand out from the rest and what you have to offer that's different from everyone else in your blog's niche.

5 Financial projections, including how much you have earned or expect to earn, your expenses, and a plan of how and when you expect your blog to be profitable. In most cases, you'll be putting this plan together once your blog is earning income, but even if it's not, it's helpful to gather this information to prepare you for the possibilities ahead.

CHAPTER
№

06

{ **MONETIZING**
Your
BLOG }

You're officially immersed in blog land: your traffic is increasing and you've become acquainted with your readers and the community your blog has created. You're probably starting to wonder about the income-earning potential of your blog. For some, their blog is a side hobby that they are happy to have simply as a creative outlet; for others, their blog adds a bit of pocket change and supplemental income. And a growing group of bloggers are able to earn up to six figures from their full-time blogging pursuits. There's an infinite range of possibilities as to what your blog could become and its potential earning power. In this chapter, we'll discuss the various methods of monetizing your blog, what to charge, how to prepare a media kit for potential ad sponsors, and how to disclose any sponsored relationships to your readers.

MEASURING TRAFFIC *and* UNDERSTANDING ANALYTICS

Before you dive in to advertising, you'll need to assess your traffic flow. Whether you use Google Analytics, IndexTools (Yahoo's analytics program), or a tool that comes with your blogging platform, it's important to have an analytics code embedded in your site so you can track your blog's stats. Each tool will differ in the way its interface appears, but all of them provide vital information that compiles your blog's traffic on a daily, weekly, monthly, or yearly basis. The most important stats and information include the following:

- The **number of unique visitors** (daily or monthly) that your blog attracts tells how big your audience (or reach) is. This stat counts each person separately. For example, 2,300 unique visitors per day means that even if someone went to your site three times that day, they'd usually be counted once in your daily statistics.

- The **average length of time** visitors spend on your site tells you whether readers are staying for a minute or ten minutes during a single visit. If readers come to your site regularly, they may take a look at new content only, while readers who are new to your site may spend some extra time perusing your archives.

- The **number of page views** tells how many of your blog's pages were viewed within a given time period (daily, weekly, or monthly). If someone visits your site and just reads the content on the front page, one page view would be counted, but if they go back to archived pages, each additional page is counted as a new page view. Usually monthly page views are the most important for your media kit. Installing a widget like LinkWithin can help increase your page views, as it provides thumbnails under each post that alert readers to past content they might be interested in.

The **bounce rate** indicates how quickly a user leaves a blog. A bounce rate under 65 percent is considered good and is worth mentioning in your media kit, as it shows that readers are staying to read your content and not clicking away too quickly.

 Traffic sources indicate where your visitors are coming from, how they find you, and what sites are linking to your blog. If you see a spike in traffic one day, this section will help you figure out where the additional traffic came from, such as from another blog or your Twitter feed.

Visitor information offers more in-depth details on your readers, including where they live, what browsers they use, and what search terms they entered to land on your site. Depending on your blog and your types of sponsors, some of these details may be helpful for your media kit.

There are also more advanced stats that these tracking tools offer, depending on what you want to know, like which posts were the most viewed; but the aforementioned are the main stats about your site that advertisers will be interested in hearing about.

RSS

RSS (Really Simple Syndication) is a very common method that many readers use to read blogs these days. Rather than going to each site separately, they get daily updates from all their favorite blogs all in one place through this subscription-style service. So, you'll want to make sure you provide an RSS link for them. You can also track your RSS feed's stats by installing FeedBurner (see Resources), which gives readers a direct link to your RSS feed and allows you to track their reading behavior. Once installed, you can see not only how many people are subscribing to your site, but also how many of them click over to your blog from the feed.

THE *ABCs* OF SEO

As a new blog, you're probably eager to get your site in front of new potential readers. With search engine optimization (SEO), you can increase the visibility of your blog by helping it to move higher up in Internet search engine results. While you can certainly hire SEO experts and consultants to optimize your site, most bloggers starting out don't have the funds to go that route. Luckily, there are things you can do on your own for no cost at all. To help increase your ranking, simply take these extra steps when composing your posts or saving your image files:

№ 1 *Index Your Site*

Your blog host may offer an option to index your site, or add it to search engine listings, so that your blog will begin to show up on search engines as soon as you start generating content. But you can also submit your URL for inclusion in Google's index through a simple online form. There's no guarantee that they'll accept it, but it's worth submitting it to their "Add your URL to Google" page.

№ 2 *Use Keyword-Rich Text When Linking*

When linking to other sites, use the actual names of artists, companies, or stores in your post. For example, if you link the rubber stamp that was used for your homemade holiday cards to the Kate's Paperie Web site, the link should say, "Rubber Stamp from Kate's Paperie" (with the words "Kate's Paperie" hyperlinked), as opposed to linking with a vague term like "click here," "buy this," or "source." Piggyback on the power of those you link to, as users are likely to search for those key words and may find your post among the listings.

№ 3 *Title and Tag with Common Phrases*

Apply titles and tags to all posts, and be sure to use keywords that are popular and common. For example, search engines will read the title "vanilla ice cream recipe" more clearly and quickly than "whipped frozen treat." Or tag your home renovation post with "kitchen" or "bedroom" instead of "dream house." You can also use Google's Keyword Tool or Wordtracker to find the optimal words or phrasing to use. Not only does this help with SEO and readers accessing your content more easily, but tagging also helps you self-organize your own blog by creating consistent tags for your content.

№ 4 Name Files with Short Dashes

When saving images to upload into your posts or naming the permalink for your post, use keywords separated by short dashes (instead of an underscore) so that it's easy for a search engine to understand. For example, an image of Clinique lipstick should be labeled "clinique-lipstick.jpeg." Also, make sure not to leave any spaces blank. If you have spaces between words instead of dashes and name the same image file above "clinique lipstick.jpeg," it will appear as "clinique%20%lipstick.jpeg" on image searches, which is not very SEO friendly.

№ 5 Crosslink

The more your site is mentioned and linked to, the higher it will rise in search results. You can use this to your benefit by linking to your old posts or past stories when applicable.

№ 6 Use SEO Plug-ins and Programs

Various plug-ins can be installed on your blog to help increase its SEO potential. Some platforms, like WordPress, offer SEO plug-ins as part of your hosting package. Other tools (like Scribe) or software (like SEOmoz) are separate and will scan your posts and make suggestions about ways you can add important keywords or subtract words that are not as effective. These services vary in pricing (usually a fee from $17 to $100 per month) based on the level of help you need. Once installed on your blog, they will also monitor your stats and give you suggestions to improve your overall SEO.

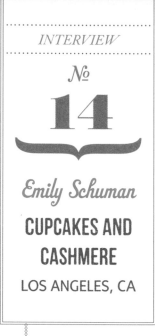

Emily Schuman

CUPCAKES AND CASHMERE

LOS ANGELES, CA

IN NEED OF A CREATIVE OUTLET from the everyday doldrums of her advertising job, Emily Schuman started her blog, Cupcakes and Cashmere, in 2008 as a place to merge her two interests: fashion and food. The ability to think editorially came naturally to her thanks to a background in media studies and sociology and stints at *Teen Vogue*, *Domino*, and AOL. However, she wanted her blog to offer a more behind-the-scenes personality and show readers things such as a real girl's wardrobe on a lazy Sunday or a tutorial on homemade ice-cream drumsticks. What started as a place for her to share her love of fashion and food now generates more than 8.3 million page views a month. Her self-made fashionista status has led to dream gigs including designing a bag for Coach, serving as a face for a Forever 21 advertising campaign, and being photographed by Garance Doré for *Glamour*. Now a full-time blogger, Emily serves as a shining example of the importance of authenticity. By only posting content she feels is the right fit, she demonstrates how originality and sincerity can lead to amazing things—like her newest book, *Cupcakes and Cashmere*.

? *How has the content of your blog changed or evolved?*

When I started, fashion blogs and food blogs were mutually exclusive, and I wanted to combine both of my interests into one site. I wasn't cooking much in the beginning, so I talked more about dining out—like a great breakfast spot or where to get sushi by the beach. On the fashion end, I'd post about new clothing lines that I thought people should know about. Since I had worked at magazines and my brain functioned editorially, the blog was a bit more editorial initially. Now I'm much more a part of my blog, as it shows a lot of my life. I think that shift to a more personal angle came from realizing that people are looking for inspiration from a real person.

A lot of your content is self-generated, including photos of your outfits or what you're cooking. How important is unique content to the success of a blog?

For me, content that readers can't find everywhere is really important. But you have to make sure that when you're posting your own content that it's also good. Photos that are out of focus or uninteresting won't help you much, even if they are your own images. So it's got to be both unique in content and strong in quality.

Readers tune in to see what you'll wear next. What's your process in choosing an outfit?

I choose what to wear based on where I'm going, what I'm doing, and what I'd actually wear there. But, because it tends to stay warm in L.A. and my readers are all over the world, I try to pay attention to the seasons so that my outfits translate to other areas. I also try to include pieces across a range of price points to achieve the look.

I think the basis of my style involves simple silhouettes. It feels clean and polished but with a bit of an eclectic, vintage touch. I'm a lot more experimental with the way I'll put things together than I used to be, and the blog has certainly helped me to be more comfortable with pushing the boundaries. In the end, every outfit has to feel like me while elevating it to something that is interesting to readers and isn't too simple. The minute you start compromising your taste and vision is when you lose that authenticity that people grow to trust.

At what point did you feel comfortable leaving your job and blogging full-time?

There was never a point of 100 percent certainty that I felt comfortable leaving my day job. I had come to a crossroads at my job at AOL. Although my position was secure, they were laying off one-third of the staff. I volunteered to be part of that group to get a bit of financial cushion from the layoff. While

- - - - ->

my parents didn't really get the whole blogging thing at the time, they were very supportive in my decision, which helped me to take the leap. Once I made the jump, I never looked back, and have not regretted it since.

? *How did the opportunities with Coach and Forever 21 come about? Did you seek them out, or did they come to you?*

I feel very lucky that I haven't had to do much outreach. All of the opportunities have come to me so far. However, I'm very careful about the relationships I form with brands—they must be brands I admire, support, and that are a natural fit for me. With Coach, they flew me and a few other bloggers out to New York for Fashion Week. We got to go behind the scenes at the Coach offices, meet with the CEO, and offer our feedback on their brand and products. The relationship grew from there, and they asked me to design a bag in collaboration with them. I was intimidated at first because I don't have any formal experience in fashion, but they walked me through the process complete with sketches, inspiration boards, and color palettes. I knew I wanted to design a bag that was classic, versatile, and unique—and ultimately something I'd love to carry.

With Forever 21, they chose five bloggers with distinct styles to be in an ad campaign. They pulled a bunch of pieces for us, and we got to put together our own ensembles. Any time you can collaborate with other bloggers and girls you admire, it's so fun. The way they worked with us and let us stick to what we'd choose on our own felt very natural and genuine.

? *Some of the items you wear on your blog have been given to you by companies. How do you deal with that editorially and acknowledge it?*

I'm consistently maintaining relationships and networking with fashion brands I love. I have meetings, attend events, see samples, and am in constant contact with the PR folks or representatives of various brands. Typically, the best relationships are when there are no assumptions. If a company sends me clothing or a handbag, I never feel obligated or required to write about them. It's not good to work with someone just because they send you something for free. It shouldn't feel forced and should be something you'd want to buy yourself or wear normally. For pieces that are given to me that I do wear and post about, I simply state that the item's been gifted to adhere to FTC regulations.

How do you generate income from your blog?

My income currently comes from three main sources: sponsored ads on my blog, affiliate links to clothing I'm wearing (where I earn a portion of the click-through sales), and earnings from my *Cupcakes and Cashmere* book.

How do you interact with your readers through Twitter and Facebook?

I try to keep the content simple and light on my blog, and then I use the other forms of social networking to share a realistic view of my life as well as behind-the-scenes stories so they can see that I'm a real person who they can relate to. I use Twitter to share information—the new boots I just got or what I had for dessert. In contrast, on Facebook, I interact a bit more and answer questions like what nail polish color I'm wearing in a post.

What's an average working day for you?

A lot of people assume blogging is really easy and that it doesn't take a lot of time, but blogging full-time really is a full-time job (and then some)! Every day is always different, but I do try to have calls and meetings daily so that I interact with people regularly. I am usually up by 6:00 A.M. I'll answer e-mails, check stats, and maintain my Twitter and Facebook pages for the first hour or two of the day. I spend a lot of the day prepping for a photo shoot and figuring out what the next day's post is going to be. If I'm going to do a food post, I have to pick out a recipe, go shopping for ingredients, create the dish, and then take photos of it. For an outfit post, I'll work on picking out the outfit—making sure to include anything new I want to show. Finally, once the photos are shot, I'll spend another few hours editing them and putting together the actual post. I'm always thinking about my blog and how something in my life can turn into a fun post and become actual content. Even though it's very demanding, and there's pressure to give fresh content daily—I'm very fortunate to do what I do, and I love every moment of it!

GETTING *Sponsors*

Every day, more and more companies are understanding the value of blogs as a way to point customers to their site to generate more sales of their products or services. When starting an advertising program, think about which companies would be a good fit as sponsors on your blog. It's always best to stick to companies or sites that you like or would buy from yourself. Look at the types of companies you already feature. For example, if you enjoy posting about natural beauty products, you could reach out to a new boutique soy candle company to let them know you'd love to help bring more customers to their site. Also, have any companies thanked you for your posts that brought them some great traffic? If they've gotten high traffic from your blog, they may be interested in your ad program.

Remember that you don't have to work with every sponsor that is interested in placing an ad on your blog, especially if their products, service, or aesthetic are not the right fit for your site. It's okay to reply with a polite e-mail telling them that you have a policy of only working with the sponsors that best fit your brand and site. Furthermore, if you convey a desire to create the best outcome for not only you but for them as well, they will usually be very understanding and appreciative that you're not just pocketing their money.

Typically, it's a good idea to wait to offer ads until your traffic is at a level that is worth your time and enticing to a sponsor. I recommend a minimum of 1,000 visitors a day or 100,000 page views a month before launching an ad program. If you're only charging $20 per month for an ad spot, once you've paid taxes on your earnings (see page 113), that income may not be worth your time. If your reader stats aren't quite there yet, you could try affiliate programs (see page 148) or offer free ads to friends with businesses or other companies you really love as a way to test out your ad program.

When you do officially launch your ad program, be sure to announce it on your blog and any other social media sites you use, like Facebook and Twitter. You can also place a simple link or graphic on your blog stating that ad space is available and how to inquire for more information. While you don't need to remind readers every week that you're now monetizing, you should spread the word every so often so potential sponsors know about this exciting new marketplace.

TYPES OF *Banner* ADS

What may seem like a small area of your site can be prime real estate for a sponsor to place a banner ad. However, unlike an ad you'd see in a magazine or newspaper, banner ads have the added benefit of taking readers directly to the sponsor's site with the click of a button. Banner ads can include one or more images, can be configured in a variety of sizes from tiny buttons to vertical towers, and be placed in various areas on your blog. You can ask your advertisers to give you static jpegs, animated gifs, or flash motion frames. Here's a look at the most common types of banner ads bloggers use.

№ 1 *Basic Banner*

You can specify the sizes and shapes of your ads, whether square, horizontal rectangle, or vertical rectangle. The width of the ads should be based on the width of your side columns to make an ad area or space that makes the most sense aesthetically. For example, if your right column is 120 pixels wide, only use and accept ads that are that width, which may include 120 × 90, 120 × 120, 120 × 240, or 120 × 600 pixels. When a reader first views your site, an "above the fold" ad is one that they would see without scrolling down the page. In comparison, a "below the fold" ad can only be seen once they've scrolled down the page. Therefore, above the fold ads are usually priced higher because of their prime placement, and are more limited in quantity due to the number of ads that can fit in that top location.

№ 2 *Leaderboard*

These rectangular ads are horizontal and squat (728 × 90 pixels, for example) and can appear in several places, commonly at the top of your site above your banner, or the bottom of your blog page. This ad space is the most coveted when placed at the top of a site, and therefore is the most costly for an advertiser. However, it's also the most in-your-face of banner options, which may be to your benefit earnings-wise, but not so much aesthetics-wise.

№ 3 *Between Posts*

A medium-size ad (around 300 × 250 pixels in size) is a common banner size to place in between posts. This is usually a pretty coveted spot, especially if it falls between your newest content, or the top two posts on your site, so the rates for an ad between posts are usually higher.

№ 4 *RSS Ads*

Readers that view your blog posts strictly through their RSS feeds won't see the ads on the side column of your blog. Therefore, you can offer advertisers ad space that will show up in the feeds above or below your post to attract those readers as well. Check with your blog platform and RSS feed host to see how to install these ads. You can also find ad options for RSS feeds through Google Ads.

TEXT LINK ADS

Text links are just like they sound: an advertiser pays you to put a link to their site on your blog. With no image attached, a text link takes up less space and looks just like a hyperlink. These links can appear in the same column as your banner ads, right below them. Deep contextual links are another form of text link, except they are part of the content of a post. For example, if you post about the acrylic paints you used for a DIY project, a sponsor can pay you to link to their paint brand.

WHAT TO *Charge*

Figuring out what to charge is usually the trickiest part of starting an ad program. There is no one secret formula out there for what the perfect pricing would be. There are many factors to consider, including your reader stats, reach, and growth since you launched, as well as what similar blogs are charging for their ads.

You may hear about ads being charged based on a CPM basis. CPM, or cost per mille (*mille* is the Latin word for 1,000), basically means the cost per 1,000 impressions. Ad networks sell ads on their sites, and larger companies

{ There is no one secret formula out there for what the perfect pricing would be. }

inquire about ad pricing based on CPM. For example, if a blog charges $1 CPM, that means the blogger would be paid $1 for every 1,000 impressions (meaning the readers that visit that blog who potentially see the ad). For a new blogger, it'll be easier to charge a flat monthly rate, since many advertisers (especially small businesses) are not set up to track CPMs.

A very basic formula to help you determine your pricing is to look at your monthly page views and divide that number by 1,000. For example, if you have 100,000 page views per month and divide that by 1,000, your base ad price (for the smallest-size ad, say 125 × 125) would be $100 per month. You can also use a blog with a larger readership to come up with your base ad rate by prorating their fees. For example, if a bigger blog in your genre generates 1,000,000 page views per month and charges $900 per month for a 125 × 125 ad, and your page views are about 100,000 per month, that's one-tenth of the other blog's readership. Therefore, you could charge one-tenth of their pricing, or $90 per month, for the small ad spot.

You should also do research on what other bloggers within your niche and with a similar level of readership are charging for a 125 × 125 ad, or something close in size. Many advertisers will shop around by requesting rates from a few blogs they're interested in to see which might offer the best value for their money. If another blog similar to yours is charging much less but has the same amount of traffic, an advertiser may very well choose that blog over yours if they are choosing solely based on budget. That's when you need to decide if you've got something to offer that the other blog doesn't, therefore making it worth it for you to stick to a slightly higher price, or if you want to be on par with their pricing. You may ask yourself, "How do I find out what other bloggers are charging?" Some blogs list their rates on their site. For those who don't, if you're friendly with them, you could simply ask. Most bloggers are open to helping others and are happy to share what they can to help you with your growing site.

Next, you may choose to tweak the base rate for the smallest ad, charging slightly more or less, for the following reasons.

Reasons to charge more:

 You've grown quickly. Maybe you've received a lot of great press in the first few months of your launch and you've seen your readership grow substantially each month.

 You have a very specific niche, so your readership is highly targeted.

 You'd prefer to accept a small number of ads on your site, so every ad will get more attention.

Reasons to charge less:

 You don't post consistently, or have a set number of times you post a week, and therefore cannot guarantee how often readers will check your site.

 You want to be an affordable option for indie businesses like Etsy shops or those who may not have big advertising budgets.

Based on the above example, I've determined that a blog with 100,000 page views could charge $100/month based on my initial formula, or $90/month if we compare it to an example of a bigger site's rates. Because my sample blog has had pretty quick growth, I'd stick to the higher of the two numbers for the 125 × 125 ad spot. Now, if you're offering a larger option as well, like 125 × 250, I'd charge anywhere from 50 percent to 75 percent more of the base $100/month price. So, that would mean $150 to $175 for the larger ad because it's twice the size. These two options (if you want to offer both sizes) can be the base price for your above-the-fold ad. See how many ads you can fit above the fold, and then offer the same sizes below the fold at a lower rate. Since below-the-fold ads don't get quite as high a placement, the pricing of those spots could be 25 percent to 40 percent less than your prime above the fold spots. So, based on this example, a 125 × 125 ad below the fold could be $60 to $75/month, and a 125 × 250 ad would be $110 to $130. To make things easier, you can offer one size only, or rotate the placement of your ads so that every ad gets to be in an above-the-fold spot each month—that way you're dealing with only one size and one price point.

You may find yourself experimenting with and tweaking your ad program rates a bit in the beginning based on the interest you receive. If you see that you're booking ads pretty quickly with your current package, keep things as-is and wait six months or until the end of the year to reassess and see if it's worth raising your rates a bit. Or, if you're not getting a ton of bookings, then lower your rate package a bit until you find a sweet spot that seems right for you. In time, you'll find a rate program that you can stick to and feel comfortable with what you're offering your sponsors. You can up your rates every year as your readership or demand grows; just be sure to raise them gradually to stay consistent with your growth. If your readership is up 10 percent from last year, you can consider raising your rates by 10 percent. It's also nice to thank longtime sponsors by giving them a smaller increase in your rate or extending the older rate a little bit longer.

№

15

April Winchell

REGRETSY

SHERMAN OAKS, CA

WHILE ETSY is known as a site for finding an array of unique handmade goods, April Winchell's blog, Regretsy, includes honest and biting commentary on the odd items people create and sell, like hand-stamped jewelry with a glaring typo, a urinal dress, a toilet paper cozy, or a batik *Star Wars* T-shirt. She finds humor in the quirky, and started her blog as a spoof of the Web site of handmade sellers. April developed her sense of humor from a young age, working as a voiceover actress for cartoons when she was eleven years old. Now, with Regretsy, she uses her innate sarcasm for both entertainment and for good. Since launching in 2009, Regretsy has raised more than $200,000 for various charities as well as for Etsy sellers who are going through rough times. She claims, "People [in the Regretsy community] aren't just mean and want to make fun of others just for the sake of it. Most are warmhearted and generous people, so I love that I can use my site based on humor to help people at the same time."

(?) *How did Regretsy begin?*

I've always had an appreciation for things that were well made and crafty, but really loved things that were offbeat and odd as well. When I discovered Etsy in 2006, a friend and I got into a habit of sending each other the terrible things we'd find on the site—it got to be really fun and hilarious. We'd give each other things like candy bowls made out of records, really ugly purses, and weird toys. Then my friend bought me an item from an Etsy seller in South Africa. It arrived with a ton of delivery issues, and when I finally got the post office to release it to me, I discovered he'd sent me a horrible white rug with a stencil of Obama on it. When I later told him how much trouble it was to get the package out of customs, he laughed and said, "I'm sorry it was such an ordeal. You have my regretsy." Then the lightbulb went off in my head. I registered the domain www.regretsy.com, and then I forgot about it. A few months later, I came across it again, and sat at my computer that weekend putting up all these crazy things from Etsy that I'd usually make fun of. I didn't think the site would last too long, and figured Etsy would be upset and have a cease-and-desist in my lap soon enough, so I figured I'd have fun with it until then.

How did people start hearing about your site?

I started Regretsy in October 2009, and within three days it had 96 million hits. Jezebel, Apartment Therapy, and MetaFilter picked it up and blogged about it within two days after my blog launched. Two days later, someone who wanted to buy the site approached me. And then two days after that, the *Wall Street Journal* and the BBC had featured it. It was crazy—this all happened within the first week!

I started off blogging anonymously because I thought people might be more intrigued by it if they didn't know who was behind it. There was an initial wave of criticism; some people thought some Hollywood studio was driving it, and others thought Diablo Cody wrote it. The initial wave of response was very positive, but also very, very negative. It was the 6,000th most popular Web site in the United States within two days, and is in the 2,000s now.

Why do you think readers enjoy your site?

Everybody has the experience of someone giving them something home-made that they hate—a bad sweater or some terrible cookies. Then, they come home from their birthday party or Secret Santa and make fun of it. It's really human, and everyone's had that experience. And my site makes fun of that through the things people choose to make.

Also, on Etsy, they don't allow you to say anything negative about any-one's work. So, I accidentally created a clearinghouse for people to vent, and I think they enjoy being able to say what they want to. I make fun of stuff simply because it's ridiculous. It turns out that I want to own these items for a different reason than the person who made it had in mind. I try to say what

----->

my initial thought is about the items I post, and it's usually also what other people are thinking. A lot of the comments and e-mails say something like "Oh my god, that's what I was thinking when I saw this!"

What was the response from Etsy?

I thought they wouldn't like it, but I wasn't initially concerned about it too much. They wrote me within two days of my blog's launch. Basically, their lawyer told me there were a few things on the site that could confuse people and make them think we were affiliated. They made it clear that they had no desire to shut me down. They just asked me to change the colors and layout, because they were really similar at the time. I didn't think of the blog being an ongoing thing initially, so I didn't think much about mocking their layout, too. But I did end up changing the layout and fonts and put a disclaimer on there that I'm not associated with Etsy.

It's ironic that even though you are making fun of sellers' products, it actually gives them a ton of traffic and sales. How has the response been from those sellers you feature?

Initially, I didn't link to the sellers, because I thought readers would harass them. But pretty quickly the sellers themselves were asking to be linked. It hadn't occurred to me that there would be value in that. But once I realized that this site could actually be a marketing tool, I got interested in a whole new way. I love seeing the way people are motivated to buy. A lot of people think you can't sell anything that is marketed in a negative or humorous way. But now sellers contact me asking to please find something in their shop to post and make fun of.

The traffic it brings sellers has been amazing. I posted about a woman who needlepoints pornographic images onto antique fabrics, because I thought the contrast between the two was hilarious. Once I posted it on Regretsy, the pillows sold out, and she got approached with a contract to create the pillows for a museum in New York. It was never my intention to keep people from selling stuff; I just found humor in some of these things they were selling.

Some people get upset and want me to take their listing down. If they want it taken down and don't make a big stink about it, I will usually comply, except in certain cases, which I mention in my FAQ section.

? *Do you monitor comments on your blog?*

I let people say what they want for the most part, unless they become disruptive or encourage harassing the seller. But I find that the community does a pretty good job of policing itself.

? *You give a portion of profits to charity every year and have raised more than $200,000 since starting your site. Why did you choose to give back in this way?*

I've always been into doing some good and working with charities. Once I saw that my site had legs and was going to be something, I quickly integrated the charity component. If it was just 100 percent snark all the time, I would have gotten tired of it by now.

Sometimes people see the site and think it's all about the nasty, mean-spirited humor, but people are more complicated and complex than that. Most of the Regretsy community is made up of warmhearted, generous people. For example, Regretsy has a team on Etsy called "April's Army." It's one of the largest teams on Etsy, with more than 2,000 sellers. Every month, I choose an Etsy seller who is struggling and needs financial and emotional support, and the team turns out in force to help them. Each team member donates at least one handmade object to the April's Army Etsy store, and the proceeds go directly to the person we've chosen to help. In the last four months, we've raised more than $25,000, helping to pay for cancer treatments, funerals, and to keep people in their homes.

? *What do you love most about blogging?*

The thing I love the most is making people laugh—that's always been my goal and my dream my whole life. I love the immediacy and the whole flash mob aspect of it. Someone wrote to me and told me about how she needed

- - - - - →

to raise money to have surgery because she didn't have insurance, so I posted about it and said, "Let's sell this girl's shop out." Immediately, her shop sold out, and she raised the money she needed to get her surgery.

? *What's your number-one piece of advice to new bloggers?*

The worst thing that you could do is to study the market and look at the sites that are successful and try and create something in that vein. Just because it's working for someone else doesn't mean that it will work for you. It has to come from something that's burning inside you, and therefore totally unique to you. Pretend there is no box or boundaries around what you can blog about, and find something that you can write about every single day.

YOUR *Media* KIT

Any potential sponsor, whether they've come to you or you've approached them, will need to know more about what your site offers them before they'll feel ready to hand over their cash. A media kit can be a simple one- to two-page PDF with your blog's logo or header that gives potential sponsors the following information.

- **Information about Your Site.** When you launched, your blog's history and growth, how often you post, what topics you cover, and why your blog adds value to your specific niche.

- **Information about You.** Your background, especially if your past work experience or what you do outside of the blog matches a potential sponsor's industry. They'd love to know that you're a mover and shaker in a particular field.

- **Site Stats.** How many unique daily readers and monthly page views you generate on average, your bounce rate (if it's low), and how many RSS subscribers you have. If you have a high page rank on Google, it's worth mentioning here, too!

- **Demographics.** Be sure to give details about your readers, including where they live, why they visit your site, and how much income they earn. This detailed information can be collected by conducting a reader survey (usually yearly) on your blog with the help of a site like SurveyMonkey.

- **Press Mentions.** If your blog has been mentioned in any magazines, online sites, or important blogs, it shows that you're making an impact with the content you provide. This bodes well for sponsors, as it shows the growth potential of your blog and that new readers are finding you from these accolades.

- **Ad Sizes.** You can offer ads ranging from simple text links and small buttons to large tower ads. Decide which options look best in the layout of your site, and offer a couple different options for sponsors. There's no need to offer every size out there, as you'll want to make it easy for you to maintain and easy for them to choose from, especially when you are just beginning.

- **Ad Location.** Whether above the fold, below the fold, in the leaderboard, or in between posts, tell sponsors where their ad will go and the various options they have to choose from.

- **Ad Costs and Duration.** List your pricing options and any discounts you offer for booking multiple months at a time. You can also decide to place a limit on how many months a sponsor can purchase at one time (for example, a three- or six-month maximum). If you decide to sell one year's worth of advertising in advance, you need to guarantee that you'll still be maintaining your blog a year from now. Also, such a long booking may not be to your advantage, as your readership may grow significantly within the year, and giving a sponsor one year's worth of your current pricing may be selling yourself short.

- **Artwork Specs.** Will you offer static jpegs, animated gifs, or both? If the idea of animated or blinking ads seems distracting to you, you can choose to allow only still jpegs with one image per ad. Specify what types of files you'll accept and any max-imum file sizes that are conducive to your blog. Usually files under 50K are good for both jpegs and animated gifs and won't bog down the load time on your site. You can also mention that you have the right to review ad artwork to make sure it's a good fit aesthetically before it goes on your blog.

- **How to Reserve.** You should always be paid up front by a spon-sor before placing their ad on your site. Otherwise, you may end up being burned by a buyer who promises to pay but never follows through. Sponsors should reserve their spot by paying for the full block of time they've committed to, whether one week, one month, or three months.

- **How to Pay.** You can decide to accept payment by check, credit card, or PayPal. Many bloggers and sponsors are comfortable with PayPal because of its ease of use. It allows you to send sponsors invoices and track your payments over time. Also, will you offer refunds or accept cancellations? Typically, it's easiest to state that once an ad is paid for, there are no cancellations or refunds allowed. That way, a sponsor can make a thoughtful and informed decision before committing to any advertising.

- **Additional Benefits.** If there are any additional benefits you can offer sponsors, be sure to add them to make your ad program even more enticing. Include information like the number of Twitter and Facebook followers you have, if you donate a per-centage of your blog revenue to charity, or if you offer sponsors the option of holding giveaways on your site.

JOINING A BLOG *Ad Network*

Similarly to how agents ease the communication between a working free-lancer and a client, ad networks help blogs access potential advertisers they wouldn't normally have contact with. There are a variety of ad networks out there, including Federated Media, Martha's Circle, BlogHer, and Glam Media, that partner with bloggers within their specific niche to offer them larger advertisers through their combined network of exposure. If you apply and are accepted into a network, be sure to check the fine print of your contract to make sure that you can also sell ads on your own. While joining a network can be helpful, you don't want it to limit the potential sponsors you could reach on your own as your blog grows. Typically, you should be blogging for at least a few months and have a growing readership before approaching such a network. While some have strict requirements on whom they'll work with and what their stats need to be, others are open to any size blog joining forces with them. All of these networks will have more information on their site about application requirements and what they can offer you.

Once you've been accepted to and joined an ad network, you'll have access to a variety of ads, many of which were discussed earlier. You may also have access to moving ads like pop-up ads, floating ads, and expanding ads. These function exactly as they sound: they appear out of nowhere, open a new page, or move across a page. You can decide whether to have these types of ads on your site, and if you choose not to, make sure you opt out with your network so that a pop-up ad that you did not want doesn't appear on your site without your knowledge.

WORKING WITH AN AGENT

As bloggers have shown their ability to become media personalities, every day more companies are looking to them to endorse their brand. The good news is bloggers don't have to secure deals with these companies on their own anymore. An influential blogger can now sign on with an agency that focuses on representing bloggers—like Digital Brand Architects—and rely on her agent to find jobs as well as negotiate fees. A blogger could score a gig to blog for her dream home decor company, pitch a TV show concept to a network, or even appear in a television commercial for her favorite brand—opportunities a blogger may not have been able to achieve on her own. But in return, a blogger will have to pay a commission (usually 10 to 20 percent) on contracts acquired through the agency.

FOUNDED IN 2003, Glam Media was created to offer new online content to women and to attract high-end advertisers to the Glam.com site. At the time, most companies were still using traditional media and were wary of advertising online. Aware of the fact that women were often in charge of the finances at home, Glam started recruiting fashion, beauty, and entertainment bloggers in 2005 to provide a network of sites that advertisers could tap into to reach their potential customers. Over the years, Glam has grown from working with 6 bloggers to partnering with more than 2,500 bloggers, and is now the eighth most visited property on the Internet. A form of ad network, Glam is a "vertical network," which represents publishers by sharing advertising options with them. Glam provides not only advertising options for its publishers (or bloggers), but also PR packages designed to help them monetize and promote their blogs. Julieta Alvarado is Glam's Senior Director of Network & Community International, and her job is to keep bloggers happy, help them generate as much revenue as possible, and continue to bring high-quality bloggers into the network. Here she shares some tips on and benefits of becoming part of a network like Glam.

? *How do bloggers earn an income through working with you? What are the different ways in which they can monetize, and what's the earning potential?*

The main source of revenue is through having a standard ad, in one of a variety of sizes, on your blog, and bloggers are compensated with an industry-standard revenue share based on the CPM that their site generates. Because we're such a big company and have a large number of campaigns and clients, we can offer ads to our bloggers that they wouldn't have access to on their own.

Clients often come to us to throw events and to help create advertorials as well. For example, Mercedes-Benz (which sponsors Fashion Week all over the world) wanted to work with a couple of our top fashion bloggers in each of the cities where Fashion Week was being held. Those bloggers got to attend and review the shows, visit and review the Mercedes-Benz lounge, and then they were compensated for creating posts about their experience. We were able to pay them a flat fee of around $5,000 for their work in addition to covering their travel and accommodations. For Toyota, we needed to recruit publishers that once owned a Toyota Camry and would be willing to talk on their blog about why they liked it and why it was a reliable car. We had some mommy bloggers who offered to talk about how it was a good family car, and the campaign included their posts, standard ads, and advertorials with full disclosure. There's usually a social media component as well where bloggers actively talk about their experiences and opinions on Facebook and Twitter. It's a way that bloggers can earn additional revenue by telling readers about products they feel passionate about. We always give them the option not to participate, and this aspect is not a requirement to work with us.

The amount that a blogger makes really varies based on their traffic and how they choose to work with us. Some make a few hundred dollars a month and some make up to $5,000 per month. We work with one very high-profile celebrity blogger who makes close to $1 million per year in revenue with us, but that's obviously the extreme, and is based on his huge readership.

? *What are the benefits to joining an ad network like yours?*

The blog industry can be so fragmented and intimidating when you're new to it that a network helps newer blogs to connect with potential advertisers that they normally wouldn't have access to. In addition to potential revenue and custom campaigns, we try and do as much PR as possible with our publishers. We'll hold events so all the bloggers can meet each other, and we try and give them spotlights in our own press mentions. For example, if we have a story being written about us for the *Wall Street Journal*, we'll pick a few bloggers

----->

to also be part of the interview. When FastCompany.com interviewed us in 2009, instead of making the article solely about Glam, we picked six of our top bloggers to be the focus of the story. We try to give them visibility, which helps them to grow their readership and hopefully get more revenue.

? *At what point can a blog join Glam? Is there a minimum traffic requirement?*

We require that you have at least 100,000 page views per month, and you have to have been blogging for over three months. We like to see blogs that are updating their content regularly and making attempts to bring unique content and grow their readership. However, if you are a newer blog but have amazing content and a look and feel that we think advertisers are going to like, we might make an exception if we think a new blog has a lot of potential.

? *What aspects should someone ask about or consider before joining an ad network?*

If I had a blog, I would want to know how reputable the company is. How long have they been in business? How do I know I'll get paid from the ads on my site? You want to make sure you're dealing with a company that is financially secure. Make sure that whomever you're working with is making an effort to expand your reach and cares about helping to grow your site.

How to PLACE AN AD ON YOUR BLOG

If you don't have any knowledge of HTML, you may be wondering how in the world you'll place these ads on your blog. While you may not have done any coding so far (especially if you're using a blog platform that makes posting super-easy), here's one reason to learn a little bit of code. The exact location where you'll apply this coding into the back end of your site will depend on your blog platform, but here is the basic information you need to embed an ad on your site if your blog platform doesn't have the functionality or plug-in to create the code for you:

Step **1** Once a sponsor sends you their artwork, check to make sure it has been set to the correct pixel size (width and length) and is in the correct format (jpeg or gif), and you've approved the artwork for your blog.

Step **2** If the file is not already named in a way that it is clear who the sponsor is, rename the ad so you can easily locate it later. For example, if you're hosting an ad from The Shade Store that's 120 × 120 pixels, you can save the ad as "Shade-Store-120-120.gif."

Step **3** Save the ad to your server if necessary and get the URL for the image's location on your server. If the advertiser chooses to host the ad image on their server, make sure they provide a URL for the location.

Step **4** Make sure you have the URL (on the sponsor's site) that the ad will link to when a reader clicks on it.

Once you have the necessary information, you'll have all the components needed to create the HTML for a blog ad. The HTML code for a blog ad is pretty simple, and once you understand the parts of it, you can copy and paste and replace information as needed. It's important to maintain the same spacing and order in this coding; otherwise you could alter the way the ad appears. You'll typically use the same code for every ad, except you'll be replacing some of the information in the quotes (" ") with new information for each ad. The typical coding for an ad might look something like this:

```
<a href="http://www.theshadestore.com/" target="_
blank"><img border=0 alt="shade store" src="http://ohjoy.
blogs.com/Shade_Store_120x120_ads.gif" width="120"
height="120" /></a>
```

<a and </a> These are the anchor points of the code, which means the beginning and end of any section of HTML. Here, your coding starts with <a, and once it's completed, it's closed by having </a> at the end.

href= This is the URL of the site you're linking to. So the sponsor's specific Web site would be placed between the quotations after href=.

target="_blank" This opens a new window or tab in your browser when the ad is clicked on. Change "_blank" to "_none" if you don't want that to happen.

img border=0 This assigns a border to the image if you want one. Otherwise, enter "0" after the equal sign.

alt="[description of the ad]" This is the image tag where the ad or sponsor can be described in a few short words. This will appear on your site if your image fails to load and is useful for helping it to appear in Internet searches.

src="[the URL for the ad image]" This is the source where the artwork image is coming from, which you'd upload to your site, or the sponsor may provide you with a link to the image from their site (see step 3 on page 145).

width="[number of pixels]" and **height="[number of pixels]"** This is the pixel width and height of the image, so make sure it matches each ad's exact dimensions.

RENEWALS

Once you're on a roll with your advertising program, you can pat yourself on the back as you see those dollars coming in. However, while you should certainly be proud of your accomplishment, maintenance will be key in keeping it going. You can keep track of the ads—when each ad block starts and ends—by creating a spreadsheet in Excel or a timeline in Google Calendar. That way, when sponsors book in advance, you know when you need to start their ad and when they're nearing the end of their ad run.

Whenever your current sponsors are near the end of their term, send them a reminder e-mail letting them know that their ads will soon expire and asking if they'd like to renew for another block. If this is their first time advertising with you, ask for their feedback and see what kind of traffic and sales they received. This is useful information for you to help gauge what your reach really is with advertisers. If they decide to renew, chances are they received some pretty good traffic. While you might assume that they'd let you know if they want to renew, most simply forget when their ad run will end on your site. Many of the sponsors on my blog renew due to their positive results—but if I didn't remind them, less than a quarter would likely remember to get in touch on their own, simply because they're busy business owners, too!

THE *Sponsored* LIFE

If you want other options to monetize other than a traditional ad, many bloggers work with sponsors to generate other forms of revenue. For example, a sponsor may offer to have you try a product in exchange for you writing your thoughts about it on your blog. These sponsored posts should still be about products that you like and use, but in this case, you are being paid to talk about your experience. For example, Jordan Ferney of Oh Happy Day! created a series of posts sponsored by Martha Stewart Living Omnimedia and Method on cleaning tips for the closet, bathroom, and kitchen. She took her own photos using the product and wrote in her own voice to keep each post as close as possible stylistically to the other content she generates on her blog. As we'll talk about later in this chapter, all sponsored posts must be disclosed to your readers—putting something as simple as "Sponsored Post" or "Sponsored by Method" in the header will do the trick.

Sponsorship can also cross over into hosted events or projects. Erin Loechner from Design for Mankind was going through a huge home renovation project for her newly purchased home in Indiana. Since she felt comfortable talking on camera, she sent a proposal to the vice president of programming for HGTV.com pitching the idea of tracking her progress through a series of Web videos on their site. HGTV accepted and compensated Erin for her regular posts on HGTV.com, and she was then able to use the coverage that attracted to get various home décor companies (like Kohler and Andersen) to donate and sponsor goods for her home. For one year, as Erin's house was being built from the ground up, she filmed weekly updates to share with HGTV fans as well as her own blog readers.

Affiliate PROGRAMS

Some companies don't have the time or desire to reach out to every blog they could potentially advertise with. Instead, they prefer to automate the process by offering an affiliate program, in which each blog is paid a commission based on the sales it generates by placing the sponsor's ad on its site. For example, if you placed a banner ad on your craft blog for a fabric supply store through an affiliate program, you'd earn a percentage (usually 5 to 10 percent) of the sales the store received from your traffic. You can apply to join an affiliate program for bigger companies, like Amazon.com, or go to sites like LinkShare, ShareASale, and Commission Junction, which work with hundreds of smaller independent companies. With the latter, you can check out the various programs they offer and, once approved to be an affiliate, get codes for ad banners and links. As with sponsored ads, you should consider whether the company you'll be helping to promote offers products or services of interest to your readers.

An affiliate program can be a great way to start offering ads when your readership isn't large enough to get sponsored ads on your own or through an ad network. It can also be a great addition to sponsored ads, since you can use affiliate ads during slower advertising months to fill in available spots. Just like sponsored ads, affiliate ads will become more successful with increasing traffic—the more readers you have, the greater the likelihood of their clicking on a link or ad and buying a product that you'd make a commission on. To keep your affiliate ads interesting, regularly check for any new ads or banner artwork the sponsor offers, so you can keep the ads looking fresh and new to your readers.

GIVEAWAYS

Everyone loves a chance to win something for free, and giveaways can be a great way to thank your readers for the time they spend visiting your home on the Internet. Blogs can choose to offer giveaways every day, every week, a handful of times a year, or not at all. As your traffic grows, you will likely be approached by companies offering to partner with you for product giveaways. Giving away something fun to one of your readers is an easy way for growing companies to get additional traffic and eyeballs to their site. Before accepting an invitation to give away a free product, make sure the item is something you'd like for yourself. If you don't like it or wouldn't use it, chances are it won't be appealing to your readers. Also, be sure to state the terms of any giveaways on your blog. What do readers have to do to enter—simply leave a comment, or do they need to visit the sponsor's site or sign up on their Facebook page? Is the giveaway open to anyone in the world, or is it limited to those located in the United States? How will you pick the winner—at random, or based on their entry? If you choose at random, you can use a third-party site like Random Number Generator (www.random.org) to pick a winner for you.

Once you start hosting giveaways on a regular basis, you'll find it requires a bit of time and maintenance to field all of the comments and entries that come pouring in. So it might make sense for you to charge sponsors for hosting a giveaway on your site. Some bloggers charge a flat fee for giveaways, while others require the business to be an existing sponsor (with a monthly banner ad)—that way, your time is compensated and the sponsor gets great traffic through your ad program. While giveaways can be a great way to draw traffic to your site, make sure you're offering them in reasonable doses so that readers aren't just coming for your giveaways and are still looking forward to the unique content you provide as well.

FULL *Disclosure*

Because your readers will grow to love and trust your opinions, you need to be honest with them any time you're compensated for posting about something, especially when it may not be obvious that you're being paid. To help make those situations a bit more clear, some rules have been put in place. The Federal Trade Commission (FTC) is an independent agency of the U.S. government whose job it is to protect consumers from being deceived by the media—which includes you, a new member. They are constantly updating the rules and regulations bloggers must follow, and foremost is making sure that bloggers provide full disclosure to their readers, particularly regarding any paid endorsements, sponsorships, or products they receive for free. Since most bloggers are not trained journalists or being guided by a large publisher, they may not be aware that they have to abide by the same standards and ethical guidelines as traditional journalists. These rules are already understood in traditional media, so the FTC is making an effort to inform bloggers of these journalistic guidelines. The FTC levies heavy fines against those who do not disclose this information. While it is clear that a company is paying you for any advertisements they may have on your blog, any product or company mentions or visuals that appear within the context of a post may not be so clear. If you are being compensated in any way through sponsorships or gifts, you must mention this either within the post, at the bottom of the post, or in the post title.

You may also find that companies want to send you products as a thank-you for your post(s) and the traffic you brought them, or would like to send you a product in hopes that you'll post about it. You may initially be jumping for joy at the thought of receiving these "blogger perks," but keep in mind that depending on what the item is—a bracelet versus a European vacation—it may be considered income, and will need to be accounted for when you file your taxes (check with an accountant about the rules in your state). Accepting a gift or a press discount after a post has been written is usually fine as long as it has no bearing on any future post, there is nothing expected of you, and it's a thank-you based on an unbiased post you've already created.

However, if you accept a product that you have not yet blogged about, there may be an expectation for you to blog about it once you receive it. Product reviews are a common practice in some niches, like beauty or food blogs,

{ It's important to stay transparent with your readers, as that builds and keeps their trust. }

where the content is based solely on trying and reviewing real products. But regardless of whether a product you received is necessary for your content, according to FTC regulations, you're required to state that the item was given to you for review.

You can choose not to accept a gift, or review a product and then send it back to the company when you're done with it. You can let companies know in a polite e-mail or note that you're happy to share things you love, but that you have a no-gifting policy. They're likely to understand and appreciate your response.

It's important to stay transparent with your readers, as that builds and keeps their trust. They'll know that whatever you post about is something you genuinely like and want to share, not simply products you're obliged to talk about because you got them for free.

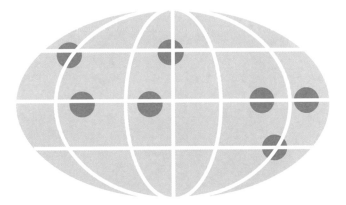

{ THE NEXT STAGE
of
BLOGGING GROWTH }

As you may have noticed from the interviews with bloggers in this book, incredible opportunities can come from starting a blog. As your blog grows, you'll find yourself dealing with both the ups and downs of blogging: You may struggle with how to balance blogging with your personal or professional life, the possibility of others copying your content, the pressure of coming up with new and exciting content while growing in leaps and bounds creatively, increasing the exposure to your business, and gaining the recognition of others in the media. In this chapter, I'll guide you through this exciting next phase of blogging growth. Whether you bring aboard a blog contributor, take your social media efforts to the next level, pitch a book idea, or go full-time as a professional blogger, this chapter covers some of the possible directions your blogging life could take as well as how to combat any hiccups along the way.

Updating YOUR BLOG'S *Design*

To keep things fresh, you'll want to change or update your blog's design every year or two. Some bloggers do this by simply updating their header, while others undergo a complete redesign. Consistency is key here. A new design should only be implemented if it still fits with the brand and tone you've already established on your blog. Think of your header like the cover of a magazine. In order for a magazine to be recognizable from month to month, the logo must remain the same, and the image behind it should feel familiar. For example, you could update the header of your flower blog each season with an image of the plants currently in bloom, but make sure that

> A new design should only be implemented if it still fits with the brand and tone you've already established on your blog.

the images are photographed consistently and interact with your logo in the same manner each time. If you change your logo and header too drastically, using different styles each time, you lose the potential to build your blog when readers keep seeing different representations of your brand. If you're considering giving your blog a full face-lift, consider any improvements in the functionality of your site that could be made at the same time, such as a navigation bar that points readers to your most popular columns. No matter what nips and tucks you do, it's always best to keep your blog's logo, aesthetic, and tone consistent with the content, niche, and brand you've worked so hard to build.

MULTIPLE BLOG DISORDER

You might have it or know someone who does. Multiple blog disorder can strike us when we find ourselves starting a new blog because we don't think our newest topic of interest fits the blog we've already established. However, you'll soon find yourself with more blogs than you can keep up with, as well as double or triple the amount of work! I, too, was struck by this plague when I launched a new food blog, Oh Joy! Eats, in 2009. I wanted to dive deeper into my foodie experiences than I had on my blog previously, and figured that separating it out would be the best way to go. Boy, was I wrong. All the years I had spent building my readership were lost when I started a new site. I had to grow my traffic all over again from the beginning, and many readers didn't even know that I had a separate food blog. I soon realized that I should have kept the two blogs combined in the first place, and once I merged them together, it not only simplified my blogging life, but also gave my readers a better sense of another one of my passions—food. Now, my food posts are some of the most popular ones on my blog.

So before you consider starting a new blog, think about whether your current readers would have any interest in the new topic you'd like to post about. How different is it? Could it fit into the overall lifestyle and aesthetic you've already created? If it's a matter of abandoning an old blog or blog name that is no longer relevant, you can always just change the name of your blog and refocus your content, if it's not working for you. Simply post about the change so readers can update their links and have your old blog address redirect to the new one. What's most important is that you don't overextend yourself—and your content—if you don't have to.

GOING *Full-Time*

The idea of blogging full-time may have once seemed incomprehensible to you, but now that the possibility is a reality, it can be really exciting and really scary all at the same time. Even though professional blogging isn't a traditional career path, or even a traditional business, you still need to take the same precautions and steps that would be involved in starting any other business. Whether you're leaving a steady paycheck from your current job or you're a stay-at-home mom turning this hobby into a full-time venture, to justify going full-time your blogging income should be able to cover, at a minimum, the cost of your living and working expenses. Calculate your total blogging expenses, including any supplies, equipment, or services you use on a regular basis. Then take a look at your personal expenses, such as your rent, groceries, utility bills, and daily expenses that may not automatically come to mind, like your yoga classes and daily frozen yogurt runs. Also, if you're losing the health benefits of a full-time job, you'll need to account for health insurance as well. Combine both sets of numbers, both business and personal, to come up with the total monthly expenses your blogging income needs to cover.

It may make the transition easier, too, if your spouse's salary can cover the ebb and flow of your freshman income, or if your partner has health insurance that will cover you, or if you have a part-time job or freelance work, or savings that will cover your living expenses for the first year. You may have to make some sacrifices as well by lowering your clothing allowance, dining out less, or moving to a less costly part of town to reduce your personal expenses. It's all worth it to do something you love for a career that you've created on your own. In time, you'll hopefully be earning a comfortable living, splurging on vacations, and saving money for retirement.

BLOGGER'S *Block*

Every blogger has moments when her creative brain goes numb and her ability to generate exciting content seems nearly impossible. When this happens to you, take a deep breath, and remember that this feeling is only temporary. Step away from the computer and try one or more of the following activities to refresh your blogging brain and get your creative juices flowing again.

Give yourself a change of scenery. As much as you may enjoy the comfort of blogging from your couch, you'll need a new environment from time to time to recharge. Try blogging from the park or a local coffee shop. Because you'll be introduced to a host of sights, smells, and sounds you don't normally witness from your usual blogging spot, a simple change in view is sure to refresh you and kick-start your blogging brain.

Take a class. Maybe you've always wanted to get your hands dirty in a pottery class or give your sweet tooth a treat with an ice cream–making class. Try a subject matter that's outside of your comfort zone and you just may find yourself with a new source of inspiration.

Move around. Getting some exercise can do wonders for your energy level and your brain cells. Go for a bike ride or take that yoga class you've always wanted to try. If you find yourself lacking in workout gusto, enlist a friend who could also use a boost, and keep each other excited and motivated to make your workouts a regular habit.

Interact with others. Although virtual interactions will be part of your day-to-day routine, physical connections are just as important. Make a coffee date with a fellow blogger or friend, or set up regular weekly brunch dates to get you out and about and catching up on life outside of the blogging world.

Reduce your number of posts. You're more likely to feel inspired and less burnt out if your number of weekly posts is a comfortable amount for you—that way, you won't feel like you're churning out posts just for the sake of it. Decrease your posting schedule from twice a day to once a day, or seven times a week to four times a week, and it's likely that you'll stay more focused while developing stronger content at the same time.

Take a blog break. Sometimes we're simply burnt out, and a vacation can be the best medicine. A week or two away from your blog just might be the rest you need. So put up a little note and tell your loyal readers you'll be taking a tiny break and will be back soon refreshed and recharged. While they may be bummed, they know you're human, too, and need to get away every so often, and you'll be back to your energetic avalanche of ideas in no time.

EXPANDING *beyond* BEING A SOLO AUTHOR

It's difficult to do everything ourselves, so it can be helpful to join forces with others or hire help when you're looking to raise the quality and quantity of the content you bring readers. The most beneficial contributors will be people who know your blog and read it regularly. When looking for someone, think about whether your contributors need to live near you or if they can work from a distance. You can seek out talented individuals by posting something on your blog, asking colleagues if they can recommend someone, or approaching a rising star (like an up-and-coming floral designer) that you think would be a good match. The most important consideration when adding someone to your team is making sure they share your vision and passion for bringing great content to your blog. You've worked long and hard to establish your voice, aesthetic, and tone, so anyone who joins your team should have a similar sensibility while also being able to bring a new point of view to the table.

CREATIVE COLLABORATION

Maybe you have a friend who's an amazing stylist who can bring your decorating ideas to life, or know a colleague who would make a mean East Coast indie band correspondent—joining forces could be a great way to promote both of your talents. Typically with collaborations, you're not bringing someone on staff or paying them like an employee. Instead, it's a mutually beneficial relationship. For example, if an old college friend is an illustrator who wants to get more editorial work, she could illustrate various posts or headers for your blog. In turn, she'll get some exposure and portfolio-building pieces that just might land her a freelance gig at her favorite magazine.

INTERNS

For a limited time, like a college semester, you can bring on an intern as a way to test out having a contributor or junior editor before diving into paying freelancers or employees. You can have them work on an existing column for your blog, research materials for a post, or even help you come up with new ideas. Usually unpaid, interns may be students getting college credit instead of a paycheck, so remember to show extra appreciation for their volunteer work, whether that means reviewing their resume or recommending them to a colleague when they've graduated and are seeking full-time work. Also, do your best to serve as a mentor for them. You can teach a budding photography student, for example, about how you conceptualize shoots for your site. If an intern applicant is no longer in school or unable to get college credit, consider how much you can afford to pay them on an hourly or weekly basis during your internship period. And, if they do well, they just may turn into a regular freelancer or employee. To find an intern, you can start with a post on your blog, but also check out your local college job boards. Depending on the expertise you'd like this intern to have, you can post something on the board within a specific major, like graphic design, to attract students on the lookout for an exciting work opportunity.

FREELANCERS

A paid freelancer can be your first step toward having regular help on your site. Freelancers are best for recurring columns, and you can pay them by the post or per hour, depending on the type of responsibilities you give them. If they're contributing a regular post once a week that they alone are

> Freelancers are best for recurring columns, and you can pay them by the post or per hour, depending on the type of responsibilities you give them.

responsible for, then paying per post will usually be easiest. How much to pay someone comes down to what you believe their time is worth and what you can afford. It's good to have a realistic idea of the time involved for the assignment you've handed them. For example, if you think $20 an hour is a fair hourly fee and that it should take them about two hours to do each post, you can offer to pay them $40 per post. If they are contributing a post once a week, then you'll be paying them about $160 a month. Payment for contributors varies from blog to blog, with some starting at $10 per post and going up to a few hundred dollars per post. So it will depend on the work involved, your budget, and your reach. Also, be sure to thank your contributors regularly and tell them when you think they're doing a great job. Freelancers like to know that they are on track and helping to grow your business. Every year, you may also consider increasing their pay, especially if your budget was a bit tight when they started. Every freelancer you hire and pay more than $600 in any one year will have to fill out a W-9 form, and you will have to file a 1099 form with the IRS to report your payments to these independent contractors.

EMPLOYEES

A paid employee is someone you're officially hiring as a staff member, on a part- or full-time basis, who will rely on you for regular paychecks. This is a big undertaking, so think wisely before bringing on anyone in this capacity. In addition to having enough work to justify a part- or full-timer, you need to be able to guarantee that your blog revenue is enough to pay their salary, as well as any yearly raises or bonuses, and health insurance, if you choose to offer it. Employees will need to be given a W-2 form at the end of every year, which your accountant or payroll service can help you with. While an employee may take a chunk out of your earnings, they can increase your productivity and efficiency and give you time to focus on growing your site and tackling other projects. With any employee—paid or not—it's also nice to thank them with bonuses, holiday gifts, or simple tokens of appreciation for their hard work and creative efforts in growing your blog.

CONTRACTS AND TRIAL PERIODS

Regardless of whether you bring on a collaborator, intern, freelancer, or paid employee, a contract is a must. Contracts establish the working relationship and expectations for both parties. The contract should state how much someone is getting paid (or not paid), how much work is involved (a weekly post or ten hours per week), when the work is due each week, the duration of the agreement (the fall semester or indefinitely), as well as any non-disclosure terms you'd like them to agree to (like how they can't duplicate the same content for their own blog or a competing blog). Finally, every contract should include the date, and both of your printed names and signatures. Also, since you won't really know someone's process and work flow until they start working with you, it's a great idea to establish a trial period (which can be anywhere from two weeks to a couple of months). This will give you a chance to see how the employee fits in with your site and work flow. At the end of the trial period, you can both assess how it's going and decide to either continue or part ways.

Once someone has shown they're a great fit for your blog, be sure to add their photo, biography, and area of expertise to the About Page of your blog so that readers know who contributes and in what ways. If your intern, employee, or contributor isn't local, the following online resources make collaborating from a distance easier: Asana or Wunderlist task management tools for teams, Google Docs file sharing, group boards on Pinterest, and shared notebooks on Evernote.

SHARING A STUDIO SPACE

If you evolve into a full-time blogger, spending much of your weekday in the virtual world, you may find that you miss being around other people. With blogging, you'll usually find yourself interacting with people from behind a screen rather than in person. If you crave support from and interaction with real-life people, a shared studio space may be something to seek out once your blog is in a position to cover these expenses. Sharing a space with other artists, creatives, or bloggers can make for a fun and motivating work environment. You can post on your blog that you're looking for a studio or studio mates. Check out local newspapers, online community boards, and rental Web sites to find places and compare locations, sizes, and pricing options.

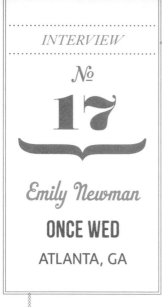

№

17

Emily Newman

ONCE WED

ATLANTA, GA

EMILY NEWMAN considers herself an accidental blogger. After her nuptials in 2008, she was looking to sell her wedding dress and realized there was a need for a Web site for brides to offer their gently worn gowns. So she launched Once Wed, an online used wedding dress listing service. Without any intention of it turning into a blog, she began including DIY tips and ideas for brides, to enhance their online experience. She soon realized that customers were enjoying the additional content as much as the dresses. A year later, she left her full-time job as a nanny to spend more time on her rapidly growing wedding blog. In 2010, she hired Joy Thigpen, a wedding photographer and stylist, as the creative director for Once Wed, who oversees all the creative content that is produced through the site. Now Emily's "accidental" blog attracts more than 4.5 million page views per month, and is a destination for brides seeking gorgeous and original inspiration for their big day.

? *At what point did you feel comfortable leaving your job to blog full-time?*

I was kind of forced to take the leap. The mom I worked for was going back to the corporate world and would need me as a full-time nanny. I knew that I couldn't balance being a full-time nanny, being there for my husband, and running the site, all at the same time. There just weren't enough hours in the day, so I decided to make a go at the blog full-time. It's stressful enough having to start a new business and make money, so I knew we needed a cushion, which included the help of my husband's full-time job and the money we had saved.

? *How did you and Joy meet and start working together?*

We met in September 2008 at a wedding event in Atlanta that a mutual friend had started. Joy had been doing wedding photography for seven years. Although she enjoyed it, she found that she cared more about the planning side and making weddings beautiful than the particulars of what lens she'd use to shoot. Styling weddings was a great combination of her skill set, and she was happy to have someone else photograph instead.

Since Atlanta is a pretty conservative market, I didn't feel as though a ton of brides understood my aesthetic, and Joy felt the same way. When we met and realized our shared interest in showing weddings in a different way, we made an instant connection as friends and collaborative partners. She started contributing to Once Wed and then became the creative director for the site officially in 2010.

? *What made you decide to bring on Joy as the creative director?*

Joy is the most talented creative I've ever been around and had the opportunity to work with. She can seriously do it all—arrange flowers, do fashion styling, take photos. The biggest lesson I've learned is to trust the person you're working with. I know I can pass off anything to her and it's going to be beautiful. From the beginning, our aesthetics were very similar. I knew it had the potential to be a great fit.

? *How much time do you spend blogging or preparing content for the blog?*

We both work about fifty to sixty hours a week for Once Wed, and that's much better than what it used to be. We had to purposely cut down our workload so that we could live life as well.

? *Nearly all your content is original. What made you decide to go that route, and how do you think it's been crucial to your success?*

When I first launched Once Wed, I would think about why magazines like *Martha Stewart Weddings* were successful—and a lot of it has to do with their unique content. When I started, a lot of wedding blogs weren't doing original content. I wanted to offer a handmade approach to brides on how they could make their wedding special. My talent didn't lie in that realm, so when I brought Joy on board to help with original content, our traffic really began to grow. Brides enjoy what we have to offer, because many of the

- - - - - >

ideas can translate into other areas of their life, even after their wedding has passed. They know they can always find something new, fresh, and original. Some of our favorite content includes when we take a mood board and bring it to life in a styled photo shoot, or create an entire place setting inspired by a painting.

What's the process of creating a new story from scratch? Do you and Joy brainstorm together first, and who is responsible for what?

Joy comes up with the inspiration boards and concepts for shoots. We discuss the concepts and ideas together and edit or remove any that don't seem like a good fit. I handle all the planning/logistics of a shoot, and Joy oversees all the creatives and the day of styling. Beyond specific shoots, I handle posting, e-mails, and sales, while Joy oversees all of the creative content.

Do you try and create stories that are trend-based?

We try to avoid trends, and tend to take things off our list if we feel like we've seen it around the blog world too much. The reason our site has grown as quickly as it has is because people know they're not going to see the same things all the time. The more you do something different and go against the trends, the more you will stand out. When we were trying to fit the mold, we'd get burnt out because we didn't feel inspired trying to keep up in that way. So now I prefer things that are different, and I like trying to come up with new things for Once Wed. But we do try and work within seasons so that it's relevant for brides.

How do you decide whom you'll hire or collaborate with on a photo shoot for the blog? Do you constantly seek out new up-and-coming talent, or do you have reliable standbys?

We love to work with other creatives. It's so refreshing to have other minds to bounce ideas off of. Sometimes it's hard to find people who we can assign a project and trust that it's going to stay in the vision that Joy came up with. We're always looking for new talent, new paper goods, photographers, makeup artists and hairstylists. We're pretty particular now because when we weren't too picky in the beginning, we weren't as happy with the end result. It's not only about style and execution; we also need people who are responsible and will answer e-mails in a timely manner or deliver files on time. We also want them to be inspired and excited about what we're creating.

With so many wedding blogs out there now, what's a tip for new bloggers who want to start a wedding blog?

Even though there are a lot of wedding blogs, you can create your own unique voice, too. Find a niche market, whether it's based on a location (like the southeast or Atlanta) or a certain type of wedding (like budget or glamorous) to help you build a very devoted audience by filling that void.

GUEST BLOGGERS

Working with guest bloggers can be a great way to bring in a rotating group of new perspectives to your blog or get help with content while you're away on vacation or maternity leave. Guest blogging is typically unpaid, as it's often a one-time thing and is mutually beneficial for both parties. You get to expose your readers to another person's perspective, while the guest blogger benefits from a new set of eyes being directed toward their site. When approaching folks to guest blog, make sure you state specifically what you'd like them to do, including the topic or theme of the post, any necessary images or layouts with the size specifications they need to provide, when you'd need the content by, and when it will run on your site. By making your request clear from the very beginning, your fellow blogger can assess if he or she has the time and interest to contribute, and is more likely to adhere to your deadlines. And, if you find that readers especially enjoy a particular guest blogger, you could consider bringing that person on as a regular contributor.

DEALING WITH *Copycats*

At some point, you may come across another blogger who seems to have gotten overly inspired by a very familiar source—you. While most bloggers don't intentionally copy content from others, the blog world is full of people who are continually inspired by the things around them, and unfortunately, sometimes that means they copy someone else's creation. If you find that someone has copied your blog content or layout, consider the following:

№ 1 *Was the Content Specific to Your Point of View or Aesthetic?*

Before getting riled up, make sure that you really have a claim to it and that you're not one of many with a similar look or content. If someone uses a polka-dotted background on their blog, it'll be tough for you to claim they copied you simply because your background is of the dotted variety as well. You can't claim a certain idea for a background unless someone pulled your exact custom-created template and used it as their own. In contrast, if someone copied your logo or header and simply replaced it with the name of their blog, that is a more direct duplication of a design that's specific to your site.

№ 2 *Was the Content Exclusive to You?*

Often PR folks send the same e-mails or give "exclusive" sneak peeks to multiple bloggers. You may not realize that a fellow blogger got the same e-mail that you did, and therefore, it's anyone's game and not yours alone to post.

№ 3 *Is It Worth Your Time?*

Before taking further steps, it's wise to choose your battles and spend time only on cases in which the infringing blogger is blatantly lifting your content or design.

№ 4 Contact the Infringer

If, after asking yourself the preceding questions, you still feel as though someone has directly copied you and that it is worth your time to stop it, your next step would be to contact the person and see if they'll remove the duplicated text or images from their site. Below are a few simple steps you can take, including consulting a lawyer, if necessary.

- **Do your research on the infringer.** Find out their name and e-mail address. Note all of the posts' URLs that are infringing on your copyright and include the posting dates.

- **Send a polite, yet direct, e-mail.** Notify the person that you found content on their site that is infringing on your copyright and ask them to remove the content immediately. Most people will take it down right away, as they have no desire to get into any legal action.

- **Contact the site that's hosting the blog.** If e-mailing the infringer isn't working, you can contact the host of the site. You can find out who hosts a blog either by looking at the URL (sometimes the host name is in the blog's URL) or by looking up their Whois record online (see Resources); Whois is a database that stores who owns a domain name or IP address. You should then alert the host site of the blog that's copying your content. For example, if Go Daddy is hosting their site, get in touch with Go Daddy's customer service and let them know your complaint and see if they can help.

- **Consult a lawyer.** If none of the above steps are working, it may be worth it to consult a lawyer about what you can do next. The lawyer will be able to put together more formal paperwork like a cease-and-desist letter, and hopefully get the infringer to take down the copied content and refrain from continuing to use the copied work.

FINDING A BLOG/LIFE *Balance*

As a full-fledged blogger, your mind will be constantly buzzing with ideas for your site. A trip to the berry farm might spur a new project for your kids' activity blog, or a visit to an art museum might trigger an idea for a new column on your art blog. Inspiration can strike at any moment, which can be both a blessing and a distraction. If you find that you have a hard time juggling your blog with your personal life, kids' schedules, and full-time job, try to dedicate certain times of the week to blogging. By now, you can probably judge how long it takes you to prepare and compose a post: including prep time, photos, editing, composing, and writing, maybe you spend thirty minutes on the shorter ones and two hours on the longer ones. If you post about ten times a week, then that's up to twenty hours per week that you might spend, based on that example. So that's twenty hours out of your week that you need to dedicate to blogging, free of other distractions or responsibilities.

When it comes to time management, knowing what needs to be tackled and when can make balancing it all easier, which holds true for lots of things in your blog business, including finances and schedules. But it is also helpful for balancing work with play and personal affairs. So if you need those twenty hours, take a look at your schedule and see when you can realistically set aside time solely for blogging. Maybe you only have nights free when you come home from your day job, in which case you can distribute that time over the course of the week or during the weekends. Or, if you're a full-time parent, plan to blog while the kids are in school or when your spouse is at home to watch them for longer periods of time. While you'll certainly find windows of free time here and there, blocking out times in advance will give you the best chance of accomplishing what you need to. It will also help you better enjoy your personal time, and make those around you feel like you're giving them your full attention. Use tools like Google Calendar or iCal, which allow you to schedule tasks to complete at specific times or on specific days to keep you on track. The beauty of these tools is that you can create different color-coded categories, such as your personal, blogging, and family schedules, which you can access from your computer, iPad, or smartphone. This means you can view everything in your life at a glance and know when you have time to blog and when you don't.

If you're the type of person who tends to lose focus easily—reading other blogs or Internet shopping during the time you're supposed to be blogging— you may want to try a self-timing time management technique or application that forces you to work in specific increments of time. The Pomodoro Technique, which was devised by Francesco Cirillo, makes you work on one task for 25 minutes at a time, with a short break afterward. By downloading the free online book, you can be guided through the process. For every four Pomodoros (25-minute blocks of time), you're allowed to take a longer break. If you'd prefer to assign yourself longer blocks of time, you can also use an application like the DUE app, which allows you to set reminders for anything on your to-do list. You can set it to remind you to start blogging at 5:00 P.M., and then to start prepping dinner at 7:00 P.M. This method gives you more control over the time between your activities. Both are examples of time management tools you can use to allot time for your blogging and personal activities, which will help you balance both worlds as seamlessly as possible.

USING YOUR BLOGGING *Skills* FOR OTHERS

While the expansion of your blog is surely a sign of success, once you've established yourself as an expert in your field or genre, it's likely that other blogs, publications, or businesses will seek out your voice to help build and strengthen their brands as well. For example, as a gardening blogger, you might receive an offer from a magazine to contribute a monthly column on urban gardening, or, as a blogger with an honest voice about the joys and tribulations of motherhood, you could be asked to write a weekly column for an online parenting site. New or established businesses may also seek your expertise to help them set up a blog or generate content for their blog, or to help them with their social media marketing.

When you are approached with these projects, first consider your availability and what your time is worth. Is it a one-time article or an ongoing project? If it's a one-time thing for a publication, they will usually pay a flat fee for your work. They may already have a going rate that they offer writers and contributors, so there may not be much room to negotiate. However, if you're approached by a company that wants to know your fee, consider how long it will take you to write or compose the article or post. If the job entails about ten hours of work per week, what's your time worth per hour? If you believe $50 per hour is fair compensation, then you should propose a weekly rate of $500 or a $2,000 per month retainer fee for your services. This fee schedule should also be applied to any projects like the consulting or social media work you'd perform for another company.

Sometimes these opportunities may not be paid, but allow you to gain some extra exposure in your field. Before accepting any new project (paid or not), also consider if it will help you grow creatively, if you can fit it into your current schedule, and if it will still be fun and interesting for you over time.

E-MAIL OVERLOAD

Pitches from PR companies, submissions from shops, sponsor inquiries, readers asking questions or advice, or fellow bloggers wanting to get together . . . you'll find your inbox growing bigger and bigger as your blog becomes more popular. It's perfectly normal to feel like you don't have the time to respond to everything. So for the questions or inquiries you get on a regular basis, it's helpful to add a frequently asked questions (FAQ) page on your blog. Here, you can answer common questions like what type of camera you use, where to eat and shop in your city, how to grow a craft blog, how you got your start, what size ad banners you accept, or how to send in a submission for review. You can set up your e-mail to auto-respond with a link to your FAQ page so that inquirers can go there directly. You should also take advantage of any mailbox filters in your e-mail program. On your FAQ or contact page, direct readers to label the subject line of their e-mail as "submission" or "advertising" so that your e-mail filter can drop it into the folder you've set up. Once you've taken these simple steps, you'll find that your e-mail will be a bit more bearable and you can respond quickly to more important and urgent e-mails.

GETTING *Published*

It seems like every blogger has a book these days (*ahem*—you're reading one of them!), but that's because blogging often serves as an amazing test forum for the ideas, services, or words of wisdom you have that make the world a better, more fun, or more entertaining place. If your blog covers a very specific topic, translating it into a print version could come rather easily, like with Adele Enersen's book, *When My Baby Dreams*—a collection of the vignettes she created and photographed around her daughter's nap-time for her blog, Mila's Daydreams. If your content is more varied, think about the most interesting topics you cover that could become a book, especially any ideas that would fill a void in the marketplace. For instance, while Angie Dudley posts about various baked goods on her blog Bakerella, it was her cake pops that garnered the most interest. Her plethora of potential ideas for cake pops turned into a best-selling book called *Cake Pops*, with her blog readers from around the world being the first to purchase copies.

Once you've narrowed down an idea for your book, you'll want to compile your concept and thoughts together for a query or proposal. A book query is usually a one-page letter introducing you and your book idea. Similar to a cover letter, it gives a publisher the gist of your concept and should include

> Once you've narrowed down an idea for your book, you'll want to compile your concept and thoughts together for a query or proposal.

three components: a hook (a concise, one-sentence tagline for your book to get a reader's interest), a mini-synopsis (a short paragraph summarizing your book idea), and your biography or credentials (what makes you an expert in the field and your blog reach, including any impressive traffic figures, awards, or accolades). The purpose of the query is to interest a publisher in hopes they'll want to know more and request a detailed proposal. If you don't have a connection to an editor, a query is often a good way to initiate contact.

A book proposal typically includes the following pieces: a sample table of contents (so that a publisher knows you have enough content to fill a whole book), a sample chapter (with full text and images, if available), market research (why your book will stand out among similar titles), and your credentials and readership (so they know the potential reach of your book). When looking for potential publishers, look for ones that produce books in the category your book would fit into—for example, fashion, cooking, or home décor. Look at the spines of your favorite like-minded books and target those publishers. If you know any bloggers who have published books already, they may be willing to introduce you to their editor. Otherwise, you can look for submission guidelines on the publisher's Web site. You can also call a publisher, find out if they take unsolicited submissions, and if so, who would be the best editor to send your query or proposal to. You never know what could happen if you don't try. While you may not get a yes right away, if an editor sees potential in your concept, they're likely to start a conversation to get the ball rolling. Having a literary agent can also make the process of pitching a proposal easier, as agents are familiar with which publishers would be the best fit for your concept and they'll make sure your proposal is the best it can possibly be. Remember, it's not about getting just any agent; you want the right agent—someone who has sold successful books in your category. Take a look at the acknowledgments in books you love and see who the author is thanking as an agent. The agents representing authors in your category would be a great place to start.

One final note: If you have even the slightest intention of turning a photo-driven blog into a book, make sure you secure permissions for all user-submitted photographs, and that you're taking or gathering images with a high enough resolution (300 dpi) for a print product. It's a major bummer to get interest from a publisher only to not have adequate material or rights.

MANY KNOW DESIGN*SPONGE as one of the very first and most well-known design blogs. Grace Bonney started her blog in 2004 as a way to chronicle the areas of the design world she loved and aspired to write about for magazines. Without any formal magazine writing experience, she decided to pen her thoughts on her blog. Since then, Design*Sponge has become an online design mecca, covering home tours, market trends, design history, movie style, business advice, city guides, new products, design show coverage, DIY projects, before and after makeovers, interviews, recipes, floral design, and entertaining. While her blog has grown much larger than

Grace Bonney

DESIGN*SPONGE

BROOKLYN, NY

she ever intended or expected it to, Grace stays true to her original mission by only generating the content she is most excited about, and presenting it in a way that is authentic to her. She knows she can't do it all, so she happily relies on a team of experts in various fields to make Design*Sponge what it is today. Now she has more than twenty freelancers and three full-time employees, a growing business empire, and a series of "design bibles" in the works, starting with her first book, *Design*Sponge at Home*. Sticking to her guns surely seems to have paid off.

? *At what point did you feel comfortable leaving your full-time job to blog full-time?*

I left my full-time PR job in 2006 when I was offered a job with *House & Garden* to be their online Web editor. I always felt more comfortable having a freelance job as a backup and for supplemental income. But when all the magazines started dropping like flies, I had no choice but to really dig in and make sure that Design*Sponge was profitable enough to support me. It was scary, but being pushed into it was probably the best way to go. I probably would have always continued to write in a freelance capacity because it made me feel safe, but the risk definitely paid off.

- - - - - ->

? *When did you decide to expand in order to grow your site?*

In 2007, I launched our first custom design and brought on the first batch of freelancers. I knew I needed to add others when I wanted to cover things I didn't know much about. I loved DIY projects and floral design but knew I wasn't qualified to talk about them, so I went to the people who knew those subjects the best and were naturally more passionate about it, and invited them to have a home on the site. And I've done that in other areas ever since. I feel incredibly honored to write alongside people who specialize in the fields I'm passionate about, but in which I know very little. This generation of readers is far more accepting of a "team of experts" and not just one all-knowing guru. I love that I get to work with people who I really admire.

? *What aspects of your business needed to be in place before you brought on your first full-time employee?*

The larger blogs I always admired seemed to either have a lot of funding or were paying people next to nothing. So for my first full-time employee, Amy Azzarito, I set up a savings account and funneled our extra earnings for a year into this "Amy account" so that if, heaven forbid, something happened with the economy, I'd still have a full year of salary to pay her. After all, she was leaving her former job to work with us.

? *Any words of advice for bloggers who want to bring on additional contributors to their site?*

First and foremost, set up a formal working relationship with a contract. It feels awkward at first, but working relationships can be sticky, and nothing sets the stage for a solid working relationship like having everyone on the same page. Once that's in place, I think it's good to add people slowly. It takes a lot of work off your plate to have help, but more work is created by having to manage them. Not only will you have to manage them as an employee, but also as someone who will have their own taste, ideas, and input about what should be on your site.

? *The bigger someone's blog gets, the more prone to negative comments it becomes. How do you deal with that?*

If jerky comments are the worst part of my job, I'm still the luckiest girl I know. After seven years of absorbing insults, complaints, and anonymous jabs online, I've built up a pretty thick skin. Mostly, I let them roll off my back because I think it's part of putting yourself out there—if you have a voice and an opinion, then people will have something to say about it.

It's a natural human instinct to want to be liked. But the desire to express myself is overpowered by the desire to be liked. I only respond to negativity when I feel someone is either a) factually inaccurate, or b) factually accurate and has pointed out something that deserves to be acknowledged and acted upon. Otherwise, I let it stand as someone's opinion. If I get the right to share mine, I don't mind letting someone else share theirs. I think it shows strength and courage to let someone really rage against you and let him or her have their moment.

Also, I see negative comments as a sign of success. You bring in a larger or different audience as you grow, and luckily in the grand scheme of things, it's a really small portion of the downsides of this business.

? *How did you translate your blog into a book idea?*

For me, the book process was about taking my time and finding the perfect publisher that understood my vision. I wanted to find a way to translate the volume of information we produce at Design*Sponge into printed form— which is tough. Most publishers want to do smaller one-topic books, but I was patient and finally found a publisher that understood that it needed to contain *everything* that made the blog popular, not just one facet. Holding out for the perfect place was really worth the wait. I'd advise anyone looking to do a book to really think hard about why you're doing it and what you want it to be. Once it's printed, it's permanent. So it's worth taking the time to get things right. That level of permanence was a big adjustment for me, coming from the Web world, where anything can be edited at any time, but it really taught me about the importance of editing closely.

- - - - - ->

The blog world changes so quickly, so I'd love to expand to other mediums like something on radio, video, or TV. Some networks have approached me for a TV show, but so far, nothing has felt like the right fit. I'm someone who has opinions, and it's not worth it to compromise if it doesn't feel authentic. When I started the site, it was because I had no goal for it and just kept doing what I wanted to do because I loved it. At the end of the day, I would rather feel comfortable with myself and my decisions over doing something just for money or a press mention. People can feel integrity or genuineness.

VIRTUAL MAGAZINES

Sometimes bloggers want to expand their blog concept into a fuller, more extensive format. With digital publishers like Issuu, starting an online magazine isn't as costly as starting a print version and can be a great way to tell a more thorough story. For example, after a few years of building his blog, Paul Lowe noticed there was a growing interest in online magazines and decided to launch one. Sweet Paul Magazine debuted in 2010 and mesmerized readers with Paul's signature styling as well as his approachable recipes and crafting ideas. Fueled by a similar motivation, more virtual magazines have popped up with bloggers at the helm, including Lonny, Rue, and Matchbook. These publications were started by bloggers who became friends online, bonded over common interests and aesthetics, and decided to work together to combine their points of view and readerships. If you decide to start an online magazine, keep in mind that you'll need more contributors and help to make it all happen. From photographers and stylists to graphic designers and advertising salespeople, it usually takes a team of experts in various fields to make a virtual magazine the best it can possibly be.

Selling PRODUCTS

If you've always wanted to run a retail store or sell your handmade plates, your blog may provide a great platform for you to do it. Because your readers are already familiar with and enjoy your aesthetic, they're a built-in customer base that will be delighted to be your first customers if you decide to open a shop. Following are two types of online shops you could start.

RETAIL SHOP HOST

If you've got an eye for creating beautiful roundups and picking out items from the Web that readers just love, hosting a retail shop may be the next extension of your blog. Being a retail shop host means creating a "shop" that you curate on your blog, and vendors typically pay you a monthly fee for featuring their items in it. You are essentially serving as a portal to showcase products you enjoy and direct readers where to buy them. Best of all, the vendors themselves handle the shipping of their products. Jan Halvorson expanded her blog, Poppytalk, with Poppytalk Handmade, a shop guided by a different theme each month that showcases her top picks of the handmade items found on Etsy. The men's fashion blog A Continuous Lean offers limited-edition products from its favorite American-made menswear partners in its hosted shop, ACL Shop. And Kelley Lilien's lifestyle blog on the fun and fabulous, Mrs. Lilien, sparked a series of collaborations with vendors in her seasonal shop, Mrs. Lilien Shoppe. Since hosting a retail shop is similar to hosting blog ads, make sure that anything you decide to carry in your shop is something you feel passionate about.

ONLINE RETAIL SHOP

Many bloggers have turned into accidental online shop owners after getting a positive response to their own homemade goods. Maybe you're an artist and have been using your illustrations to narrate your daily adventures, but readers have been begging for prints of your work, or you've been making adorable baby booties on your craft blog and get inquiries all the time from readers who would rather buy yours than make them on their own.

Nikole Herriott wrote about various inspirations and moments in her life for two years on her blog, Forty-Sixth at Grace, also photographing and posting the handcrafted wooden cake pedestals and spoons her father made. Due to increased interest in these, she opened an online shop, Herriott Grace, with her dad and now gives readers updates via e-mail and her blog. Now the items sell out within hours of posting. Online marketplaces like Etsy and Big Cartel make it easy to set up an online shop, providing you with a storefront, shopping cart, and payment processing. Marketplaces usually charge a flat monthly fee as well as take a small percentage of your sales. If you decide to dive into this type of retail business, remember that this is a whole other enterprise in itself. You'll be responsible for packing and shipping orders as well as answering customer service inquiries and complaints. These tasks aren't the most fun, and will take up additional time on top of blogging, so while this is a great way to share your talent with others, proceed with caution and weigh all your options before diving in.

GIVING BACK

After a lot of hard work generating great content, some bloggers may start to notice a growth in income, to their surprise and delight. Because of their ability to reach people in this unique way, many choose to donate a portion of their proceeds to a cause (or two) that's near and dear to their hearts. If you're in a position to give some of your profits to a charity, you can choose to donate an amount based on your yearly income, or at certain times of the year, or when catastrophic world events occur. If you decide to give back, make sure that your readers know about your do-good spirit. You can mention your charitable giving on your About page, in your media kit, or when you're looking to raise money for a specific event. Chances are, both your sponsors and readers will want to help out in any way they can. However you spread the word, what's most important is that you're helping others who are less fortunate, and giving to a cause you feel passionate about supporting.

YOUR BLOG'S *Future*

From book deals and accolades in the press to a creative outlet from your 9-to-5 job to new friends from all over the world—blogging has the potential to bring a plethora of exciting things into your life. The best thing about being a blogger is having the opportunity to create whatever you want—your blog can be about any subject that interests you the most, and it can be as big or as small or as private or public as you want it to be. How many other careers in life allow such flexibility? Always remember that the growth of a

{ With passion in your heart, patience in your blog's development, and a lot of hard work, your content will grow and readers will come. }

blog is organic and will be different for everyone. With passion in your heart, patience in your blog's development, and a lot of hard work, your content will grow and readers will come. No one ever accomplished incredible things by just sitting around. The numerous possibilities and successes of blogging are up to you to create and make happen. Having a blog is something I never expected to do or turn into a career, and now I can't imagine my life without it. So go ahead—your very own blog journey awaits you!

Resources

BLOGS

For more information on the bloggers and businesses interviewed:

Altitude Design Summit, www.altitude
summit.com

Amy Blogs Chow, www.amyblogschow
.tumblr.com

Caitlin McGauley, www.caitlinmcgauley
.com/blog

Color Collective, www.color-collective
.blogspot.com

Cupcakes and Cashmere, www.cupcakes
andcashmere.com

Design*Sponge, www.designsponge.com

Emily Henderson, www.stylebyemily
henderson.com

Geninne's Art Blog, www.geninne.com

Girl Crush, www.girlcrush.la

Glam Media, www.glammedia.com

From Me to You, www.fromme-toyou
.tumblr.com

kate spade new york, www.katespade.com

Made by Joel, www.madebyjoel.com

Once Wed, www.oncewed.com

Public School, www.gotopublicschool.com

The Purl Bee, www.purlbee.com

Regretsy, www.regretsy.com

Rockstar Diaries, www.tazaandhusband
.com

AD NETWORKS & REPS

BlogHer Publishing, www.blogherads.com

Digital Brand Architects, www.thedigital
brandarchitects.com

Federated Media, www.federatedmedia.net

Glam Media, www.glammedia.com

Martha's Circle, marthascircle.martha
stewart.com

rewardStyle, www.rewardstyle.com

ADVERTISING TOOLS

DoubleClick for Publishers (Google Ad
Manager), www.google.com/dfp/info/sb

Google AdSense, www.google.com/adsense

Google Analytics, www.google.com/analytics

Google Keyword Tool, adwords.google.com/
select/KeywordToolExternal

AFFILIATE AD PROGRAMS

Beso, www.beso.com

BlogAds, www.blogads.com

Commission Junction, www.cj.com

Google AdSense, www.google.com/adsense

LinkShare, www.linkshare.com

RewardStyle, www.rewardstyle.com

ShareASale, www.shareasale.com

BLOG PLATFORMS & HOSTS

Blogger, www.blogger.com

Moveable Type, www.movabletype.org

Squarespace, www.squarespace.com

Tumblr, www.tumblr.com

TypePad, www.typepad.com

WordPress, www.wordpress.com

CLASSES

Blogshop, www.blogshopla.wordpress.com

Jessica Sprague's Online Classes, www
.jessicasprague.com

Photoshop, www.photoshop.com/people

Skillshare, www.skillshare.com

CONFERENCES & EVENTS

Altitude Design Summit, www.altitude
summit.com

Blogfest, www.blogfest2011.com

BlogHer, www.blogher.com/conferences

BlogWorld, www.blogworldexpo.com

Design Bloggers Conference, design-bloggers-conference.com

Food Blog Camp, www.foodblogcamp.com

Lucky Magazine's Fashion and Beauty Blogger Conference (Fabb), luckymag.com/blogconference

IMAGE BOOKMARKING

Evernote, www.evernote.com

FFFFOUND!, www.ffffound.com

Flickr, www.flickr.com

Gimme Bar, www.gimmebar.com

Pinterest, www.pinterest.com

Svpply, www.svpply.com

Wantworthy, www.wantworthy.com

IPHONE CAMERA APPS

8mm, www.nexvio.com

Grid Lens, www.bucketlabs.net

Instagram, www.instagram.com

ShakeItPhoto, www.bananacameraco.com

ONLINE SHOP SYSTEMS

Big Cartel, www.bigcartel.com

Etsy, www.etsy.com

Goodsie, www.goodsie.com

PayPal, www.paypal.com

Shopify, www.shopify.com

PROTECTING YOUR WORK

Berne Copyright Convention, www.copyright.gov/title17/92appii.html

Copyscape, www.copyscape.com

Creative Commons, www.creativecommons.org

TinEye, www.tineye.com

Tynt, www.tynt.com

U.S. Copyright Office, www.copyright.gov

U.S. Patent and Trademark Office, www.uspto.gov

Whois, www.whois.net

RSS TOOLS

FeedBurner, www.feedburner.com

Google Reader, www.google.com/reader

SEO TOOLS

Scribe, www.scribeseo.com

SeoBook, www.seobook.com

SEOmoz, www.seomoz.com

Top Rank, www.toprankblog.com

SOCIAL NETWORKING

Facebook, www.facebook.com

Flickr, www.flickr.com

Google+, plus.google.com

LinkWithin, www.linkwithin.com

Twitter, www.twitter.com

Vimeo, www.vimeo.com

YouTube, www.youtube.com

TIME MANAGEMENT & ORGANIZATION

Asana, www.asana.com

Billings, www.marketcircle.com/billings

Due, www.dueapp.com

Google Calendar, www.google.com/calendar

Pomodoro Technique, www.pomodorotechnique.com

TeuxDeux, www.teuxdeux.com

TWITTER APPLICATIONS

HootSuite, www.hootsuite.com

Selective Tweets, www.facebook.com/selectivetwitter

TwitPic, www.twitpic.com

WIDGETS & OTHER TOOLS

NetworkedBlogs, www.facebook.com/networkedblogs

Random Number Generator, www.random.org

SurveyMonkey, www.surveymonkey.com

Index

Acknowledgments

To my editors, Meg Mateo Ilasco and Kate Woodrow, and my agent, Stefanie Von Borstel, for your guidance and enthusiastic support of my first solo book project from the very beginning. To Grace Bonney for your kind foreword and believing in the need for this book, to Lab Partners for your beautiful illustrations, and to Meg Mateo Ilasco for making my words look good with your book design and for starting the "Inc" series that I am so proud to be a part of. Big thanks to all of the inspiring bloggers and interviewees featured in this book for sharing your stories and experiences: April Winchell, Amy Cao, Caitlin McGauley, Cecilia Liu, Emily Henderson, Emily Newman, Emily Schuman, Gabrielle Blair, Geninne Zlatkis, Grace Bonney, Jamie Beck, Jay B Sauceda, Joel Henriques, Joelle Hoverson, Julieta Alvarado, Lauren Willhite, Naomi Davis, and Wendy Withers. I learned so much from all of you.

To my longtime friend, Beth Stellato, for sparking my interest in blogging so many years ago and giving me the push I needed to start a hobby that turned into a life-changer. To my husband, Bob, for your never-ending support, encouragement, feedback, humor, and love throughout my work and in our lives together. To my parents for always believing in me. And finally, to my daughter, Ruby—who was in my belly when I wrote this book—thanks for pushing me through my deadlines with your swift kicks and gentle pokes. You've brought a whole new set of inspirations to my world.